INTRODUCTION TO PRINCIPIA LATINA,
Part I.

THE YOUNG BEGINNER'S

FIRST LATIN BOOK:

CONTAINING THE

RUDIMENTS OF GRAMMAR, EASY GRAMMATICAL QUESTIONS
AND EXERCISES, WITH VOCABULARIES.

DESIGNED AS A STEPPING-STONE TO

DR. WM. SMITH'S PRINCIPIA LATINA, Part I.

For the Use of Young Children of both Sexes.

LONDON:
JOHN MURRAY, ALBEMARLE STREET.
1879.

In the interest of creating a more extensive selection of rare historical book reprints, we have chosen to reproduce this title even though it may possibly have occasional imperfections such as missing and blurred pages, missing text, poor pictures, markings, dark backgrounds and other reproduction issues beyond our control. Because this work is culturally important, we have made it available as a part of our commitment to protecting, preserving and promoting the world's literature. Thank you for your understanding.

PREFACE.

This book has been drawn up by Mr. M. Gutteridge, B.A., Head-Master of the Gravesend Proprietary School, under the superintendence of Dr. William Smith, and is intended for the use of young children of both sexes, beginning Latin at a very early age. It claims to be the easiest Latin book that can be placed in the hands of beginners, and is designed strictly as an Introduction to PRINCIPIA LATINA, Part I. It therefore contains the same paradigms for Declension and Conjugation, and the same words in the Exercises and Vocabularies, so that pupils passing on from this book to the Principia will recognize forms and words with which they are already familiar, and will thus find their progress rendered much easier. Whether it is advisable to begin Latin at so early an age as is now the usual practice, it is unnecessary to discuss; but as the Principia has been pronounced by most teachers the easiest book for learning Latin, it is advisable that very young children should have a suitable introduction to it, and not be compelled to use works containing different paradigms for Declension and Conjugation, and a different Vocabulary. In the case of children beginning Latin at a somewhat later period, they may commence at once with the Principia without passing through this Introduction.

The work is divided into four parts: the Grammatical Forms, Questions on the Grammar, Exercises, and Vocabularies.

I. *The Grammatical Forms.*—These contain the declensions of the Nouns, Adjectives, Numerals and Pronouns, and the conjugation of the verb Sum and of the Active Voice of the Verb. The Declensions are given with the greatest possible brevity, all rare and irregular forms being omitted. The Cases are arranged both as in the ordinary grammars and as in the Public School Latin Primer, so that the book can be used with equal advantage by those who prefer either the old or the modern arrangement. Though the grammatical forms are printed consecutively, it is recommended that they should be prepared *pari passu* with the Questions, Exercises, and Vocabularies.

II. *Questions on the Grammar.*—These are purposely very full, so as to test thoroughly the knowledge of the pupil in the grammatical forms of the Nouns and Adjectives and of the Indicative Mood of the Active Verb. In these days of examination it will be an advantage to the pupil to have been trained from the very first to answer printed questions. Questions have not been given on the Pronouns and on the other Moods of the Verb; for though these forms may be committed to memory by young children, their usage had better be deferred till the pupil commences the Principia.

III. *The Exercises.*—Each Exercise is divided into two parts; the Introductory or (A) part, with its corresponding (A) Vocabulary, which should be done before the (B) Exercises are attempted. The Exercises include only the Nominative and Accusative Cases of the Noun and Adjective, and only the Third Person Singular and Plural of the Tenses of the Indicative Mood of the Verb. All practical teachers know the difficulty which young children have in constructing the simplest sentences in a foreign language, and especially in a language with inflexions like the Latin. It has therefore been thought advisable to familiarize them with the simplest construction of a sentence, without introducing the Genitive, Dative, and Ablative Cases, which they will find when they come to the Principia.

The Exercises on the *Adjective together with the Noun* are the most numerous, because it is here that the beginner finds the most difficulty, more especially when the Noun and Adjective are not of the same Declension.

Two main features of the book are the principle of teaching by frequent repetition and the *correspondence* of two or more Exercises, the same words being for the most part used in each, so that the pupil's attention may be concentrated on the inflexion of the word, which is the only new feature of the new sentence. (See Exercises I., X., and XXII.)

Alliteration has been employed, when practicable, that the smoothness of the sentence may aid the learner.

These Exercises can be either written after school or read off in class *vivâ voce*: if they are thus written, they should be first said under the guidance of the master, as a mistake once written down becomes impressed on the mind and is difficult to eradicate.

IV. *The Vocabularies.*—The words in the Vocabularies are, with four exceptions, the same as in Principia Latina, Part I., and should be committed to memory before the Exercise is attempted. Accordingly they are divided into two parts, (A) and (B), corresponding to the Exercises. A very limited Vocabulary is given, so that special attention may be devoted to inflexion and to the agreement of the words in the sentences, the exact force of the epithets and the meaning of the sentences being matters of secondary importance.

The great object of the work is to ground the pupil thoroughly in the Grammatical Forms, and to enable him to understand the construction of the simplest sentences and the agreement of the Noun and Adjective. However long this may take, the time will not be lost; but when it has been completely attained, this little book will probably be worn out, and may then, with advantage, be replaced by Principia Latina, Part I.

CONTENTS.

PART I.
	PAGE
GRAMMATICAL FORMS :—	
The Cases arranged as in the Ordinary Grammar	1
The Cases arranged as in the Public School Primer	[1]
The Verb	17

PART II.
QUESTIONS ON THE GRAMMATICAL FORMS.	28

PART III.
EXERCISES	54

PART IV.
VOCABULARIES	92
INDEX TO VOCABULARIES :—	
Latin Words	99
English Words	102

PART I.

GRAMMATICAL FORMS.

THE CASES ARRANGED AS IN THE ORDINARY GRAMMARS.

I.—THE ALPHABET. PARTS OF SPEECH.

1. *Alphabet.*—The Latin Alphabet consists of 25 letters, the same as the English without *W*.

A, B, C, D, E, F, G, H, I, J, K, L, M, N, O, P,
a, b, c, d, e, f, g, h, i, j, k, l, m, n, o, p,
Q, R, S, T, U, V, X, Y, Z.
q, r, s, t, u, v, x, y, z.

The letters are divided into Vowels and Consonants.

The Vowels are *a, e, i, o, u, y*. The remaining letters are Consonants.

The Diphthongs are *ae, oe, au*, which are in common use, and *eu, ei, ui*, which occur in only a few words.

The diphthongs *ae, oe*, are pronounced as *ē*.

A Long Syllable has the mark (¯) over the vowel. A Short Syllable has the mark (˘) over the vowel.

2. *Parts of Speech.*—There are eight parts of speech in the Latin language.

1. Substantive, or Noun.	3. Pronoun.	6. Preposition.
2. Adjective.	4. Verb.	7. Conjunction.
	5. Adverb.	8. Interjection.

There is no article in the Latin language: hence the Latin mensă means not only *table*, but also *a table* and *the table*.

LAT. FOR BEG. I.

II.—Pronunciation.

The letters in Latin were probably pronounced as follows:—

VOWELS AND DIPHTHONGS.

Latin	ā	=	English	*a* in f*a*ther.
,,	ă	=	,,	*fir*st *a* in *a*way, or *a* in vill*a*.
,,	ē	=	,,	*ai* in p*ai*n.
,,	ae	=	,,	*ai* in p*ai*n.
,,	oe	=	,,	*ai* in p*ai*n.
,,	ĕ	=	,,	*e* in m*e*n.
,,	ī	=	,,	*i* in mach*i*ne.
,,	ĭ	=	,,	*i* in p*i*ty.
,,	ō	=	,,	*o* in gl*o*ry.
,,	ŏ	=	,,	*o* in t*o*p.
,,	ū	=	,,	*u* in r*u*le.
,,	ŭ	=	,,	*u* in f*u*ll.
,,	au	=	,,	*ow* in p*ow*er.
,,	eu	=	,,	Latin ĕ followed quickly by Latin ŭ (differs little from present pronunciation).
,,	ei	=	,,	Latin ĕ followed quickly by Latin i (differs little from *ei* in pl*ai*n).

CONSONANTS.

Latin c, ch		=	English	*k*.
,,	g	=	,,	*g* in *g*et.
,,	s	=	,,	*s* in *s*in.
,,	t (ratio)	=	,,	*t* in ca*t*, not *sh*, as in na*t*ion.
,,	j	=	,,	*y* in *y*ard.
,,	v	=	,,	*v*.
,,	z, ph, th	=	,,	*z, ph, th*.

Latin *s* between two vowels = (sometimes) English *s* in ro*s*e, *e.g.* 'ro*s*a.'

III.—SUBSTANTIVES OR NOUNS.

Nouns are declined by *Number* and *Case*.

There are two Numbers: *Singular* and *Plural*.

There are six Cases: *Nominative, Genitive, Dative, Accusative, Vocative, Ablative*.

There are three Genders: *Masculine, Feminine*, and *Neuter*.

Nouns which may be either Masculine or Feminine are called *Common*.

There are five Declensions, distinguished by the endings of the Genitive Case.

	I.	II.	III.	IV.	V.
Gen. Sing.	ae	ī	ĭs	ûs	ĕī
Gen. Plur.	Ā-rum	Ō-rum	{-um / Ī-um}	Ŭ-um	Ē-rum

The *Stem* is that part of the word which remains after the changeable endings are taken away.

The *Stems* of Nouns can be ascertained by taking away the terminations *um* or *rum* of the Genitive Plural. Hence the final letter of the Stem is in—

	I.	II.	III.	IV.	V.
	A	O	consonant or I	U	E

IV.—THE FIRST OR A DECLENSION.

The Nominative Singular of Nouns of the First Declension ends in ă.

	Sing.			Plur.	
Nom.	Mens-ă (*fem.*)	*a table*	Mens-ae,	*tables*
Gen.	Mens-ae,	*of a table*	Mens-ārum,	*of tables*
Dat.	Mens-ae,	*to or for a table*	Mens-īs,	*to or for tables*
Acc.	Mens-am,	*a table*	Mens-ās,	*tables*
Voc.	Mens-ă,	*O table*	Mens-ae,	*O tables*
Abl.	Mens-ā,	*by, with, or from a table*	Mens-īs,	*by, with, or from tables*

GENDER.—All Nouns of the First Declension are Feminine, unless they designate males: as, nauta, *a sailor*.

V.—The Second or O Declension.

The Nominative Singular of Masculine Nouns of the Second Declension ends in **ŭs** and **ĕr**, and of Neuter Nouns in **um**.

A. *Masculine.*

1.

	Sing.			Plur.	
Nom.	Dŏmĭn-ŭs,	a lord	Dŏmĭn-ī,	lords
Gen.	Dŏmĭn-ī,	of a lord	Dŏmĭn-ōrum,	of lords
Dat.	Dŏmĭn-ō,	to or for a lord	Dŏmĭn-īs,	to or for lords
Acc.	Dŏmĭn-um,	a lord	Dŏmĭn-ōs,	lords
Voc.	Dŏmĭn-ĕ,	O lord	Dŏmĭn-ī,	O lords
Abl.	Dŏmĭn-ō,	by, with, or from a lord.	Dŏmĭn-īs,	by, with, or from lords.

2.

Nom.	Măgistĕr,	a master	Măgistr-ī,	masters
Gen.	Măgistr-ī,	of a master	Măgistr-ōrum,	of masters
Dat.	Măgistr-ō,	to or for a master	Măgistr-īs,	to or for masters
Acc.	Măgistr-um,	a master	Măgistr-ōs,	masters
Voc.	Măgistĕr,	O master	Măgistr-ī,	O masters
Abl.	Măgistr-ō,	by, with, or from a master.	Măgistr-īs,	by, with, or from masters.

3.

Nom.	Puĕr,	a boy	Puĕr-ī,	boys
Gen.	Puĕr-ī,	of a boy	Puĕr-ōrum,	of boys
Dat.	Puĕr-ō,	to or for a boy	Puĕr-īs,	to or for boys
Acc.	Puĕr-um,	a boy	Puĕr-ōs,	boys
Voc.	Puĕr,	O boy	Puĕr-ī,	O boys
Abl.	Puĕr-ō,	by, with, or from a boy.	Puĕr-īs,	by, with, or from boys.

B. *Neuter.*

	Sing.			Plur.	
Nom.	Regn-um,	a kingdom	Regn-ă,	kingdoms
Gen.	Regn-ī,	of a kingdom	Regn-ōrum,	of kingdoms
Dat.	Regn-ō,	to or for a kingdom	Regn-īs,	to or for kingdoms
Acc.	Regn-um,	a kingdom	Regn-ă,	kingdoms
Voc.	Regn-um,	O kingdom	Regn-ă,	O kingdoms
Abl.	Regn-ō,	by, with, or from a kingdom.	Regn-īs,	by, with, or from kingdoms.

NOTE.—The Nominative, Accusative, and Vocative of all Neuter Nouns are the same.

GENDER.— Most Nouns in **ŭs** are Masculine, but names of trees are Feminine; as, mālŭs, *an apple-tree.*

VI.—The Third or Consonant and I Declension.

The Nominative Singular of Nouns of the Third Declension ends in various letters. Their stems end in some consonant or i.

A. *Masculine and Feminine Nouns.*

I. Stem ending in a Consonant.

	Sing.		Plur.	
Nom.	Trăb-s (*f.*),	*a beam*	Trăb-ĕs,	*beams*
Gen.	Trăb-ĭs,	*of a beam*	Trăb-um,	*of beams*
Dat.	Trăb-ī,	*to or for a beam*	Trăb-ĭbŭs,	*to or for beams*
Acc.	Trăb-em,	*a beam*	Trăb-ĕs,	*beams*
Voc.	Trăb-s,	*O beam*	Trăb-ĕs,	*O beams*
Abl.	Trăb-ĕ,	*by, with,* or *from a beam.*	Trăb-ĭbŭs,	*by, with,* or *from beams.*

II. Stem ending in I.

	Sing.		Plur.	
Nom.	Host-ĭs (*c.*),	*an enemy*	Host-ĕs,	*enemies*
Gen.	Host-ĭs,	*of an enemy*	Host-ĭum,	*of enemies*
Dat.	Host-ī,	*to or for an enemy*	Host-ĭbŭs,	*to or for enemies*
Acc.	Host-em,	*an enemy*	Host-ĕs,	*enemies*
Voc.	Host-ĭs,	*O enemy*	Host-ĕs,	*O enemies*
Abl.	Host-ĕ,	*by, with,* or *from an enemy.*	Host-ĭbŭs,	*by, with,* or *from enemies.*

B. *Neuter Nouns.*

I. Stem ending in a Consonant.

	Sing.		Plur.	
Nom.	Ŏpŭs,	*a work*	Ŏpĕr-ă,	*works*
Gen.	Ŏpĕr-ĭs,	*of a work*	Ŏpĕr-um,	*of works*
Dat.	Ŏpĕr-ī,	*to or for a work*	Ŏpĕr-ĭbŭs,	*to or for works*
Acc.	Ŏpŭs,	*a work*	Ŏpĕr-ă,	*works*
Voc.	Ŏpŭs,	*O work*	Ŏpĕr-ă,	*O works*
Abl.	Ŏpĕr-ĕ,	*by, with,* or *from a work.*	Ŏpĕr-ĭbŭs,	*by, with,* or *from works.*

II. Stem ending in I.

	Sing.		Plur.	
Nom.	Măr-ĕ,	*the sea*	Măr-ĭă,	*seas*
Gen.	Măr-ĭs,	*of the sea*	Măr-ĭum,	*of seas*
Dat.	Măr-ī,	*to or for the sea*	Măr-ĭbŭs,	*to or for seas*
Acc.	Măr-ĕ,	*the sea*	Măr-ĭă,	*seas*
Voc.	Măr-ĕ,	*O sea*	Măr-ĭă,	*O seas*
Abl.	Măr-ī,	*by, with,* or *from the sea.*	Măr-ĭbŭs,	*by, with,* or *from seas.*

VII.—THE FOURTH OR U DECLENSION.

The Nominative Singular of Masculine and Feminine Nouns of the Fourth Declension ends in **ŭs**, and of Neuter Nouns in **ŭ**.

1.

	Sing.			Plur.	
Nom.	Gráid-ŭs (m.),	a step	Gráid-ūs,	steps
Gen.	Gráid-ūs,	of a step	Gráid-ŭum,	of steps
Dat.	Gráid-ŭi,	to or for a step	Gráid-ĭbus,	to or for steps
Acc.	Gráid-um,	a step	Gráid-ūs,	steps
Voc.	Gráid-ŭs,	O step	Gráid-ūs,	O steps
Abl.	Gráid-ū,	by, with, or from a step.	Gráid-ĭbus,	by, with, or from steps.

2.

	Sing.			Plur.	
Nom.	Gĕn-ū (n.),	a knee	Gĕn-ŭa,	knees
Gen.	Gĕn-ūs,	of a knee	Gĕn-ŭum,	of knees
Dat.	Gĕn-ū,	to or for a knee	Gĕn-ĭbus,	to or for knees
Acc.	Gĕn-ū,	a knee	Gĕn-ŭa,	knees
Voc.	Gĕn-ū,	O knee	Gĕn-ŭa,	O knees
Abl.	Gĕn-ū,	by, with, or from a knee.	Gĕn-ĭbus,	by, with, or from knees.

NOTE.—Some Nouns of the Fourth Declension make the *Dat.* and *Abl. Pl.* in -ŭbus: as, ăc-ŭbus, from ăc-ŭs, *a needle*; port-ŭbus, from port-ŭs, *a harbour*, and others.

GENDER.—Most Nouns of the Fourth Declension in **ŭs** are Masculine, but a few are Feminine: as, mănŭs, *a hand*; dŏmŭs, *a house*.

VIII.—THE FIFTH OR E DECLENSION.

The Nominative Singular of Nouns of the Fifth Declension ends in **ēs**.

	Sing.			Plur.	
Nom.	Dĭ-ēs,	a day	Dĭ-ēs,	days
Gen.	Dĭ-ēi,	of a day	Dĭ-ērum,	of days
Dat.	Dĭ-ēi,	to or for a day	Dĭ-ēbus,	to or for days
Acc.	Dĭ-em,	a day	Dĭ-ēs,	days
Voc.	Dĭ-ēs,	O day	Dĭ-ēs,	O days
Abl.	Dĭ-ē,	by, with, or from a day.	Dĭ-ēbus,	by, with, or from days.

GENDER.—All Nouns of the Fifth Declension are Feminine except dĭēs, which is either Masculine or Feminine in the Singular, and always Masculine in the Plural; and mĕrīdĭēs, *midday*, which is always Masculine.

IX.—Adjectives of the First and Second Declensions.

Adjectives in ŭs, ă, um, or ĕr, (ĕ)ră, (ĕ)rum, are declined in the Masculine and Neuter like Nouns of the Second Declension, and in the Feminine like Nouns of the First Declension: as, bŏnŭs, bŏnă, bŏnum, *good;* nĭgĕr, nigră, nigrum, *black;* tĕnĕr, tĕnĕră, tĕnĕrum, *tender.*

1.

	Sing. M.	F.	N.	Plur. M.	F.	N.
Nom.	Bŏn-ŭs	bŏn-ă	bŏn-um	Bŏn-ī	bŏn-ae	bŏn-ă
Gen.	Bŏn-ī	bŏn-ae	bŏn-ī	Bŏn-ōrum	bŏn-ārum	bŏn-ōrum
Dat.	Bŏn-ō	bŏn-ae	bŏn-ō	Bŏn-īs	bŏn-īs	bŏn-īs
Acc.	Bŏn-um	bŏn-am	bŏn-um	Bŏn-ōs	bŏn-ās	bŏn-ă
Voc.	Bŏn-ĕ	bŏn-ă	bŏn-um	Bŏn-ī	bŏn-ae	bŏn-ă
Abl.	Bŏn-ō	bŏn-ă	bŏn-ō	Bŏn-īs	bŏn-īs	bŏn-īs

Nĭgĕr is declined in the Masculine like Măgistĕr.

2.

	M.	F.	N.	M.	F.	N.
Nom.	Nĭg-ĕr	nigr-ă	nigr-um	Nigr-ī	nigr-ae	nigr-ă
Gen.	Nigr-ī	nigr-ae	nigr-ī	Nigr-ōrum	nigr-ārum	nigr-ōrum
Dat.	Nigr-ō	nigr-ae	nigr-ō	Nigr-īs	nigr-īs	nigr-īs
Acc.	Nigr-um	nigr-am	nigr-um	Nigr-ōs	nigr-ās	nigr-ă
Voc.	Nĭg-ĕr	nigr-ă	nigr-um	Nigr-ī	nigr-ae	nigr-ă
Abl.	Nigr-ō	nigr-ă	nigr-ō	Nigr-īs	nigr-īs	nigr-īs

Tĕnĕr is declined in the Masculine like Puĕr.

3.

	M.	F.	N.	M.	F.	N.
Nom.	Tĕnĕr	tĕnĕr-ă	tĕnĕr-um	Tĕnĕr-ī	tĕnĕr-ae	tĕnĕr-ă
Gen.	Tĕnĕr-ī	tĕnĕr-ae	tĕnĕr-ī	Tĕnĕr-ōrum	tĕnĕr-ārum	tĕnĕr-ōrum
Dat.	Tĕnĕr-ō	tĕnĕr-ae	tĕnĕr-ō	Tĕnĕr-īs	tĕnĕr-īs	tĕnĕr-īs
Acc.	Tĕnĕr-um	tĕnĕr-am	tĕnĕr-um	Tĕnĕr-ōs	tĕnĕr-ās	tĕnĕr-ă
Voc.	Tĕnĕr	tĕnĕr-ă	tĕnĕr-um	Tĕnĕr-ī	tĕnĕr-ae	tĕnĕr-ă
Abl.	Tĕnĕr-ō	tĕnĕr-ă	tĕnĕr-ō	Tĕnĕr-īs	tĕnĕr-īs	tĕnĕr-īs

The only Adjectives declined like tĕnĕr are the following:—

asper, ĕra, ĕrum, *rough*	prosper, ĕra, ĕrum, *prosperous*
lacer, ĕra, ĕrum, *torn*	liber, ĕra, ĕrum, *free*
miser, ĕra, ĕrum, *wretched.*	

With all Adjectives in fer and ger: as—

| lănĭger, ĕra, ĕrum, *wool-bearing* | ŏpĭfer, ĕra, ĕrum, *help-bringing.* |

X.—ADJECTIVES OF THE THIRD DECLENSION.

I. ADJECTIVES OF THREE TERMINATIONS end in ĕr, rĭs, rĕ, and are declined like Nouns of the Third Declension. They have three terminations in the Nominative and Vocative Singular only: as, ācĕr, ācris, ācrĕ, *sharp;* cĕlĕr, cĕlĕris, cĕlĕrĕ, *swift.*

	Sing.			Plur.	
	M.	F.	N.	M. and F.	N.
Nom.	Ācĕr	ācris	ācrĕ	Ācrēs	ācrĭă
Gen.	Ācris	ācris	ācris	Ācrĭum	ācrĭum
Dat.	Ācrī	ācrī	ācrī	Ācrĭbŭs	ācrĭbŭs
Acc.	Ācrem	ācrem	ācrĕ	Ācrēs	ācrĭă
Voc.	Ācĕr	ācris	ācrĕ	Ācrēs	ācrĭă
Abl.	Ācrī	ācrī	ācrī	Ācrĭbŭs	ācrĭbŭs

II. ADJECTIVES OF TWO TERMINATIONS are declined like Nouns of the Third Declension. They have two terminations in the Nominative, Vocative, and Accusative only. They include—

    1. Adjectives ending in ĭs: as, tristĭs (*masc.* and *fem.*), tristĕ (*neut.*), *sad.*
    2. Comparatives, ending in ĭor, ĭus: as, mĕlĭŏr (*masc.* and *fem.*), mĕlĭŭs (*neut.*), *better.*

1.

	Sing.		Plur.	
	M. and F.	N.	M. and F.	N.
Nom.	Trist-ĭs	trist-ĕ	Trist-ēs	trist-ĭă
Gen.	Trist-ĭs	trist-ĭs	Trist-ĭum	trist-ĭum
Dat.	Trist-ī	trist-ī	Trist-ĭbŭs	trist-ĭbŭs
Acc.	Trist-em	trist-ĕ	Trist-ēs	trist-ĭă
Voc.	Trist-ĭs	trist-ĕ	Trist-ēs	trist-ĭă
Abl.	Trist-ī	trist-ī	Trist-ĭbŭs	trist-ĭbŭs

2.

	M. and F.	N.	M. and F.	N.
Nom.	Mĕlĭŏr	mĕlĭŭs	Mĕlĭŏr-ēs	mĕlĭŏr-ă
Gen.	Mĕlĭŏr-ĭs	mĕlĭŏr-ĭs	Mĕlĭŏr-um	mĕlĭŏr-um
Dat.	Mĕlĭŏr-ī	mĕlĭŏr-ī	Mĕlĭŏr-ĭbŭs	mĕlĭŏr-ĭbŭs
Acc.	Mĕlĭŏr-em	mĕlĭŭs	Mĕlĭŏr-ēs	mĕlĭŏr-ă
Voc.	Mĕlĭŏr	mĕlĭŭs	Mĕlĭŏr-ēs	mĕlĭŏr-ă
Abl.	Mĕlĭŏr-ĕ or ī	mĕlĭŏr-ĕ or ī	Mĕlĭŏr-ĭbŭs	mĕlĭŏr-ĭbŭs

III. ADJECTIVES OF ONE TERMINATION are of various endings and declined like Nouns of the Third Declension: as, fēlix, *fortunate.*

	Sing.		Plur.	
	M. and F.	N.	M. and F.	N.
Nom.	Fēlix	fēlix	Fēlĭc-ēs	fēlĭc-ĭă
Gen.	Fēlĭc-ĭs	fēlĭc-ĭs	Fēlĭc-ĭum	fēlĭc-ĭum
Dat.	Fēlĭc-ī	fēlĭc-ī	Fēlĭc-ĭbŭs	fēlĭc-ĭbŭs
Acc.	Fēlĭc-em	fēlix	Fēlĭc-ēs	fēlĭc-ĭă
Voc.	Fēlix	fēlix	Fēlĭc-ēs	fēlĭc-ĭă
Abl.	Fēlĭc-ī or ĕ	fēlĭc-ī or ĕ	Fēlĭc-ĭbŭs	fēlĭc-ĭbŭs

XI.—ADJECTIVES AND NOUNS DECLINED TOGETHER.

I. Feminine Adjective declined along with Feminine Noun, both of First Declension.

Sing.

Nom.	Parvă mensă,	a small table
Gen.	Parvae mensae,	of a small table
Dat.	Parvae mensae,	to or for a small table
Acc.	Parvam mensam,	a small table
Voc.	Parvă mensă,	O small table
Abl.	Parvā mensā,	by, with, or from a small table.

Plur.

Nom.	Parvae mensae,	small tables
Gen.	Parvārum mensārum,	of small tables
Dat.	Parvīs mensīs,	to or for small tables
Acc.	Parvās mensās,	small tables
Voc.	Parvae mensae,	O small tables
Abl.	Parvīs mensīs,	by, with, or from small tables.

II. Masculine Adjectives declined along with Masculine Nouns, both of Second Declension.

(A.)

Sing.

Nom.	Bŏnŭs dŏmĭnŭs,	a good lord
Gen.	Bŏnī dŏmĭnī,	of a good lord
Dat.	Bŏnō dŏmĭnō,	to or for a good lord
Acc.	Bŏnum dŏmĭnum,	a good lord
Voc.	Bŏnĕ dŏmĭnĕ,	O good lord
Abl.	Bŏnō dŏmĭnō,	by, with, or from a good lord.

Plur.

Nom.	Bŏnī dŏmĭnī,	good lords
Gen.	Bŏnōrum dŏmĭnōrum,	of good lords
Dat.	Bŏnīs dŏmĭnīs,	to or for good lords
Acc.	Bŏnōs dŏmĭnōs,	good lords
Voc.	Bŏnī dŏmĭnī,	O good lords
Abl.	Bŏnīs dŏmĭnīs,	by, with, or from good lords.

(B.)

Sing.

Nom.	Bŏnŭs pŭĕr,	a good boy
Gen.	Bŏnī pŭĕrī,	of a good boy
Dat.	Bŏnō pŭĕrō,	to or for a good boy
Acc.	Bŏnum pŭĕrum,	a good boy
Voc.	Bŏnĕ pŭĕr,	O good boy
Abl.	Bŏnō pŭĕrō,	by, with, or from a good boy.

Plur.

Nom.	Bŏnī pŭĕrī,	good boys
Gen.	Bŏnōrum pŭĕrōrum,	of good boys
Dat.	Bŏnīs pŭĕrīs,	to or for good boys
Acc.	Bŏnōs pŭĕrōs,	good boys
Voc.	Bŏnī pŭĕrī,	O good boys
Abl.	Bŏnīs pŭĕrīs,	by, with, or from good boys.

ADJECTIVES AND NOUNS.

III. Neuter Adjective declined along with Neuter Noun, both of Second Declension.

Sing.
Nom.	Magnum regnum,	a great kingdom
Gen.	Magnī regnī,	of a great kingdom
Dat.	Magnō regnō,	to or for a great kingdom
Acc.	Magnum regnum,	a great kingdom
Voc.	Magnum regnum,	O great kingdom
Abl.	Magnō regnō,	by, with, or from a great kingdom.

Plur.
Nom.	Magnă regnă,	great kingdoms
Gen.	Magnōrum regnōrum,	of great kingdoms
Dat.	Magnīs regnīs,	to or for great kingdoms
Acc.	Magnă regnă,	great kingdoms
Voc.	Magnă regnă,	O great kingdoms
Abl.	Magnīs regnīs,	by, with, or from great kingdoms.

IV. Nouns of Third Declension, and Adjectives of First and Second Declensions, declined together.

1. Magnŭs Dux,—a great leader.

	Sing.		Plur.
Nom.	Magnŭs dux		Magnī dŭcēs
Gen.	Magnī dŭcĭs		Magnōrum dŭcum
Dat.	Magnō dŭcī		Magnīs dŭcĭbŭs
Acc.	Magnum dŭcem		Magnōs dŭcēs
Voc.	Magnĕ dux		Magnī dŭcēs
Abl.	Magnō dŭcĕ		Magnīs dŭcĭbŭs.

2. Bŏnă Lex,—a good law.

Nom.	Bŏnă lex		Bŏnae lēgēs
Gen.	Bŏnae lēgĭs		Bŏnārum lēgum
Dat.	Bŏnae lēgī		Bŏnīs lēgĭbŭs
Acc.	Bŏnam lēgem		Bŏnās lēgēs
Voc.	Bŏnă lex		Bŏnae lēgēs
Abl.	Bŏnă lēgĕ		Bŏnīs lēgĭbŭs

3. Răpĭdum Flūmĕn,—a rapid river.

Nom.	Răpĭdum flūmĕn		Răpĭdă flūmĭnă
Gen.	Răpĭdī flūmĭnĭs		Răpĭdōrum flūmĭnum
Dat.	Răpĭdō flūmĭnī		Răpĭdīs flūmĭnĭbŭs
Acc.	Răpĭdum flūmĕn		Răpĭdă flūmĭnă
Voc.	Răpĭdum flūmĕn		Răpĭdă flūmĭnă
Abl.	Răpĭdō flūmĭnĕ		Răpĭdīs flūmĭnĭbŭs

V. Adjectives of Third Declension, declined with Nouns of First, Second, and Third Declensions.

1. Cĕlĕrĭs Săgittă,—*a swift arrow.*

	Sing.	Plur.
Nom.	Cĕlĕrĭs săgittă	Cĕlĕrēs săgittae
Gen.	Cĕlĕrĭs săgittae	Cĕlĕrum săgittārum
Dat.	Cĕlĕrī săgittae	Cĕlĕrĭbŭs săgittīs
Acc.	Cĕlĕrem săgittam	Cĕlĕrēs săgittās
Voc.	Cĕlĕrĭs săgittă	Cĕlĕrēs săgittae
Abl.	Cĕlĕrī săgittă	Cĕlĕrĭbŭs săgittīs

2. Tristĕ Proelĭum,—*a sad battle.*

	Sing.	Plur.
Nom.	Tristĕ proelĭum	Tristĭă proelĭă
Gen.	Tristĭs proelĭī	Tristĭum proelĭōrum
Dat.	Tristī proelĭō	Tristĭbŭs proelĭīs
Acc.	Tristĕ proelĭum	Tristĭă proelĭă
Voc.	Tristĕ proelĭum	Tristĭă proelĭă
Abl.	Tristī proelĭō	Tristĭbŭs proelĭīs

3. Fēlix Hŏmo,*—*a happy man.*

	Sing.	Plur.
Nom.	Fēlix hŏmo	Fēlĭcēs hŏmĭnēs
Gen.	Fēlĭcĭs hŏmĭnĭs	Fēlĭcĭum hŏmĭnum
Dat.	Fēlĭcī hŏmĭnī	Fēlĭcĭbŭs hŏmĭnĭbŭs
Acc.	Fēlĭcem hŏmĭnem	Fēlĭcēs hŏmĭnēs
Voc.	Fēlix hŏmo	Fēlĭcēs hŏmĭnēs
Abl.	Fēlĭcī or ĕ hŏmĭnĕ	Fēlĭcĭbŭs hŏmĭnĭbŭs

* NOTE.—Nouns the stems of which end in ŏn or ōn (ĭn) have simply o in the *Nom. Sing.*: as, lĕo, lĕōn-ĭs, *a lion;* hŏmo, hŏmĭn-is, *a man.*

XII.—COMPARISON OF ADJECTIVES.

Adjectives have three Degrees of Comparison: Positive, Comparative, and Superlative: as,

Positive.	Comparative.	Superlative.
Altŭs, *high.*	Altĭŏr, *higher.*	Altissĭmŭs, { *highest, most high,* or *very high.*

The Comparative is formed by adding *ĭŏr* and the Superlative by adding *issĭmŭs* to the Positive, after taking away the termination of the Genitive Singular: as,

Posit. Nom.	Gen.		Comp.	Sup.
Altŭs,	Alt-ī,	*high,*	Alt-ĭŏr,	Alt-issĭmŭs.
Lĕvĭs,	Lĕv-ĭs,	*light,*	Lĕv-ĭŏr,	Lĕv-issĭmŭs.
Fēlix,	Fēlĭc-ĭs,	*fortunate,*	Fēlĭc-ĭŏr,	Fēlĭc-issĭmŭs.
Prūdens,	Prūdent-ĭs,	*prudent,*	Prūdent-ĭŏr,	Prūdent-issĭmŭs.

COMPARISON OF ADJECTIVES.

The Comparative is declined on p. 8 (měl-ĭŏr). The Superlative is declined like bŏnus, bŏna, bŏnum.

EXCEPTIONS.— I. Adjectives ending in ĕr form the Superlative in rĭmŭs: as,

Posit.	Gen.		Comp.	Sup.
pulchĕr,	pulchr-ī,	*beautiful*,	pulchr-ĭor,	pulcher-rĭmŭs.
lībĕr,	lībĕr-ī,	*free*,	lībĕr-ĭor,	līber-rĭmŭs.
ācĕr,	ācr-ĭs,	*sharp*,	ācr-ĭor,	ācer-rĭmŭs.
cĕlĕr,	cĕlĕr-ĭs,	*swift*,	cĕlĕr-ĭor,	cĕler-rĭmŭs.

Also vĕtŭs (*Gen.* vĕtĕr-ĭs), *old*, has a Superlative, vĕter-rĭmŭs.

II. The following six Adjectives ending in ĭlĭs form their Superlative in lĭmŭs:

Posit.		Comp.	Sup.
făcĭlĭs,	*easy*,	făcĭl-ĭor,	făcĭl-lĭmŭs.
diffĭcĭlĭs,	*difficult*,	diffĭcĭl-ĭor,	diffĭcil-lĭmŭs.
sĭmĭlĭs,	*like*,	sĭmĭl-ĭor,	sĭmil-lĭmŭs.
dissĭmĭlĭs,	*unlike*,	dissĭmĭl-ĭor,	dissĭmil-lĭmŭs.
grăcĭlĭs,	*thin*,	grăcĭl-ĭor,	grăcil-lĭmŭs.
hŭmĭlĭs,	*low*,	hŭmĭl-ĭor,	hŭmil-lĭmŭs.

IRREGULAR COMPARISON.

Posit.		Comp.	Sup.
bŏnus,	*good*,	mĕlĭor,	optĭmŭs.
mălus,	*bad*,	pĕjor,	pessĭmŭs.
magnus,	*great*,	măjor,	maxĭmŭs.
parvus,	*small*,	mĭnor,	mĭnĭmŭs.
multus,	*much*,	plūs (*see below*),	plūrĭmŭs.

Plūs, the comparative of multus, is declined as follows:—

	Singular. Neut. only.	Plural. Masc. and Fem.	Neut.
Nom.	Plūs	Plūrēs	Plūră
Gen.	Plūrĭs	Plūrĭum	Plūrĭum
Dat.	Plūrī	Plūrĭbŭs	Plūrĭbŭs
Acc.	Plūs	Plūrēs	Plūră
Abl.	Plūrĕ	Plūrĭbŭs	Plūrĭbŭs

XIII.—The Numerals.

Cardinal Numerals denote number simply or absolutely: as, ūnŭs, *one*; dŭŏ, *two*; trĕs, *three*.

Ordinal Numerals denote numbers regarded as forming parts of a series: as, prīmŭs, *first*; sĕcŭndŭs, or altĕr, *second*. They are declined regularly as adjectives.

Arabic Symbols.	Roman Symbols.	Cardinals.	Ordinals.
1	I	ūnus	prīmus.
2	II	dŭŏ	sĕcundus *or* altĕr.
3	III	trĕs	tertĭus.
4	IV	quattŭŏr (quătŭŏr)	quartus.
5	V	quinquĕ	quintus.
6	VI	sex	sextus.
7	VII	septem	septĭmus.
8	VIII	octŏ	octāvus.
9	IX	nŏvem	nōnus.
10	X	dĕcem	dĕcĭmus.
11	XI	undĕcim	undĕcĭmus.
12	XII	duŏdĕcim	duŏdĕcĭmus.
13	XIII	trĕdĕcim	tertĭus dĕcĭmus.
14	XIV	quattuordĕcim	quartus dĕcĭmus.
15	XV	quindĕcim	quintus dĕcĭmus.
16	XVI	sēdĕcim	sextus dĕcĭmus.
17	XVII	septemdĕcim	septĭmus dĕcĭmus.
18	XVIII	duŏdēvīgintī	duŏdēvīcĕsĭmus.
19	XIX	undēvīgintī	undēvīcĕsĭmus.
20	XX	vīgintī	vīcĕsĭmus.
100	C	centum	centēsĭmus.
1000	M *or* CIↃ	millĕ	millēsĭmus.

The Cardinal Numerals, except ūnŭs, dŭŏ, trĕs, are not declined. Mīlle is declined only in the Plural. Ūnŭs is declined like bŏnŭs, except that the Genitive Singular (M., F., and N.) is ūnīŭs, and the Dative Singular (M., F., and N.) is ūnī.

Dŭŏ, *two*, trĕs, *three*, and millĭă, *thousands*, are declined as follows:—

	M.	F.	N.	M. and F.	N.	N.
Nom.	Dŭ-ŏ	dŭ-ae	dŭ-ŏ	Trĕs	trĭă	Millĭă
Gen.	Dŭ-ōrum	dŭ-ārum	dŭ-ōrum	Trĭum	trĭum	Millĭum
Dat.	Dŭ-ōbŭs	dŭ-ābŭs	dŭ-ōbŭs	Trĭbŭs	trĭbŭs	Millĭbŭs
Acc.	Dŭ-ŏs *or* dŭ-ŏ	dŭ-ās	dŭ-ŏ	Trĕs *or* trīs	trĭă	Millĭă
Abl.	Dŭ-ōbŭs	dŭ-ābŭs	dŭ-ōbŭs	Trĭbŭs	trĭbŭs	Millĭbŭs

XIV.—THE PRONOUNS.

I. PERSONAL PRONOUNS.

1. *Pronoun of the First Person.*

	Sing.			Plur.	
Nom.	Ĕgŏ,	I	Nōs,		we
Gen.	Mĕī,	of me	Nostrī or nostrum,		of us
Dat.	Mĭhi,	to or for me	Nōbīs,		to or for us
Acc.	Mē,	me	Nōs,		us
Abl.	Mē,	by, with, or from me.	Nōbīs,		by, with, or from us.

2. *Pronoun of the Second Person.*

	Sing.			Plur.	
Nom.	Tū,	thou	Vōs,		ye
Gen.	Tŭī,	of thee	Vestrī or vestrum,		of you
Dat.	Tĭbi,	to or for thee	Vōbīs,		to or for you
Acc.	Tē,	thee	Vōs,		you
Voc.	Tū,	O thou	Vōs,		O ye
Abl.	Tē,	by, with, or from thee.	Vōbīs,		by, with, or from you.

3. *Pronoun of the Third Person.*

For the Pronoun of the Third Person, *he, she, it,* Ĭs, ĕă, ĭd, is usually employed. (See p. 16.)

II. REFLECTIVE PRONOUN OF THE THIRD PERSON.

The Reflective Pronoun refers to the Subject of the sentence, and cannot therefore have a Nominative case.

Sing. and Plur.

Gen.	Sŭī,	of himself, herself, itself, or themselves.
Dat.	Sĭbi,	to or for himself, herself, itself, or themselves.
Acc.	Sē or sēsē,	himself, herself, itself, or themselves.
Abl.	Sē or sēsē,	by or from himself, herself, itself, or themselves.

There are no distinct reflective forms in the 1st and 2nd persons; the different cases of *ego* and *tu* being used reflectively: as, mĕī, *of myself;* tĭbi, *to thyself,* etc.

III. Possessive Pronouns.

These are formed from the First and Second Personal and the Third Reflective Pronouns, and are declined as adjectives:

M.	F.	N.	
Měus,	měa,	měum,	*my* or *mine*.
Tŭus,	tŭa,	tŭum,	*thy* or *thine*.
Noster,	nostra,	nostrum,	*our, ours*.
Vester,	vestra,	vestrum,	*your, yours*.
Sŭus,	sŭa,	sŭum,	*his, her, its, their*.

IV. Demonstrative Pronouns.

1. Hic, haec, hoc, *this (near me)*; pl. *these*.

	Sing.				Plur.		
	M.	F.	N.		M.	F.	N.
Nom.	Hic	haec	hoc		Hī	hae	haec
Gen.	Hūjus				Hōrum	hārum	hōrum
Dat.	Huic				Hīs		
Acc.	Hunc	hanc	hoc		Hōs	hās	haec
Abl.	Hōc	hāc	hōc		Hīs		

2. Istě, istă, istŭd, *that (near you), that of yours*; pl. *those*.

Nom.	Istě	istă	istŭd		Istī	istae	istă
Gen.	Istīus				Istōrum	istārum	istōrum
Dat.	Istī				Istīs		
Acc.	Istum	istam	istŭd		Istōs	istās	istă
Abl.	Istō	istā	istō		Istīs		

3. Illě, illă, illŭd, *that, that yonder*; pl. *those*.

Nom.	Illě	illă	illŭd		Illī	illae	illă
Gen.	Illīus				Illōrum	illārum	illōrum
Dat.	Illī				Illīs		
Acc.	Illum	illam	illŭd		Illōs	illās	illă
Abl.	Illō	illā	illō		Illīs		

PRONOUNS.

V. DETERMINATE, RELATIVE, AND INTERROGATIVE PRONOUNS.

1. Ĭs, eă, ĭd, *he, she, it, that,* referring to the former part of a sentence.

	Sing. M.	F.	N.	Plur. M.	F.	N.
Nom.	Ĭs	eă	ĭd	Iĭ	eae	eă
Gen.	Ějus			Eōrum	eārum	eōrum
Dat.	Eĭ			Iĭs *or* eĭs		
Acc.	Eum	eam	ĭd	Eōs	eās	eă
Abl.	Eō	eă	eō	Iĭs *or* eĭs		

2. Ĭdem, eădem, ĭdem, *the same.*

	Nom. Ĭdem	eădem	ĭdem	Iĭdem	eaedem	eădem
Gen.	Ějusdem			Eōrundem	eārundem	eōrundem
Dat.	Eĭdem			Iĭsdem *or* eĭsdem		
Acc.	Eundem	eandem	ĭdem	Eōsdem	eāsdem	eădem
Abl.	Eōdem	eādem	eōdem	Iĭsdem *or* eĭsdem		

3. Ipsĕ, ipsă, ipsum, *self, himself, herself, itself.*

	M.	F.	N.	M.	F.	N.
Nom.	Ipsĕ	ipsă	ipsum	Ipsī	ipsae	ipsă
Gen.	Ipsīus			Ipsōrum	ipsārum	ipsōrum
Dat.	Ipsī			Ipsīs		
Acc.	Ipsum	ipsam	ipsum	Ipsōs	ipsās	ipsă
Abl.	Ipsō	ipsā	ipsō	Ipsīs		

4. Relative—Quī, quae, quŏd, *who* or *which.*

	M.	F.	N.	M.	F.	N.
Nom.	Quī	quae	quŏd	Quī	quae	quae
Gen.	Cūjus			Quōrum	quārum	quōrum
Dat.	Cuī			Quĭbus *or* quīs		
Acc.	Quem	quam	quŏd	Quōs	quās	quae
Abl.	Quō	quā	quō	Quĭbus *or* quīs		

5. Interrogative—Quĭs or quī, quae, quĭd or quŏd, *who? which? what?*

	M.	F.	N.	M.	F.	N.
Nom.	Quĭs *or* quī	quae	quĭd *or* quŏd	Quī	quae	quae
Gen.	Cūjus			Quōrum	quārum	quōrum
Dat.	Cuī			Quĭbus *or* quīs		
Acc.	Quem	quam	quĭd *or* quŏd	Quōs	quās	quae
Abl.	Quō	quā	quō	Quĭbus *or* quīs		

PART I.

GRAMMATICAL FORMS.

THE CASES ARRANGED AS IN THE PUBLIC SCHOOL PRIMER.

I.—THE ALPHABET. PARTS OF SPEECH.

1. *Alphabet.*—The Latin Alphabet consists of 25 letters, the same as the English without *W*.

A, B, C, D, E, F, G, H, I, J, K, L, M, N, O, P,
a, b, c, d, e, f, g, h, i, j, k, l, m, n, o, p,
Q, R, S, T, U, V, X, Y, Z.
q, r, s, t, u, v, x, y, z.

The letters are divided into Vowels and Consonants.

The Vowels are *a, e, i, o, u, y*. The remaining letters are Consonants.

The Diphthongs are *ae, oe, au*, which are in common use, and *eu, ei, ui*, which occur in only a few words.

The diphthongs *ae, oe*, are pronounced as *ē*.

A Long Syllable has the mark (¯) over the vowel. A Short Syllable has the mark (˘) over the vowel.

2. *Parts of Speech.*—There are eight parts of speech in the Latin language.

    1. Substantive, or Noun.   5. Adverb.
    2. Adjective.   6. Preposition.
    3. Pronoun.   7. Conjunction.
    4. Verb.   8. Interjection.

There is no article in the Latin language: hence the Latin **mensă** means not only *table*, but also *a table* and *the table*.

II.—PRONUNCIATION.

The letters in Latin were probably pronounced as follows:—

VOWELS AND DIPHTHONGS.

Latin			English	
"	ā	=	English	*a* in f*a*ther.
"	ă	=	"	*first a* in *a*way, or *a* in vill*a*.
"	ē	=	"	*ai* in p*ai*n.
"	ae	=	"	*ai* in p*ai*n.
"	oe	=	"	*ai* in p*ai*n.
"	ĕ	=	"	*e* in m*e*n.
"	ī	=	"	*i* in mach*i*ne.
"	ĭ	=	"	*i* in p*i*ty.
"	ō	=	"	*o* in gl*o*ry.
"	ŏ	=	"	*o* in t*o*p.
"	ū	=	"	*u* in r*u*le.
"	ŭ	=	"	*u* in f*u*ll.
"	au	=	"	*ow* in p*ow*er.
"	eu	=	"	Latin ĕ followed quickly by Latin ŭ (differs little from present pronunciation).
"	ei	=	"	Latin ĕ followed quickly by Latin i (differs little from *ai* in pl*ai*n).

CONSONANTS.

Latin c, ch	=	English *k*.
" g	=	" *g* in *g*et.
" s	=	" *s* in *s*in.
" t (ratio)	=	" *t* in ca*t*, not *sh*, as in na*t*ion.
" j	=	" *y* in *y*ard.
" v	=	" *v*.
" z, ph, th	=	" *z, ph, th*.

Latin *s* between two vowels = (sometimes) English *s* in ro*s*e, *e.g.* 'rosa.'

III.—SUBSTANTIVES OR NOUNS.

Nouns are declined by *Number* and *Case*.

There are two Numbers: *Singular* and *Plural*.

There are six Cases: *Nominative, Vocative, Accusative, Genitive, Dative, Ablative*.

There are three Genders: *Masculine, Feminine*, and *Neuter*.

Nouns which may be either Masculine or Feminine are called *Common*.

There are five Declensions, distinguished by the endings of the Genitive Case.

	I.	II.	III.	IV.	V.
Gen. Sing.	ae	ī	ĭs	ūs	ĕī
Gen. Plur.	Ā-rum	Ō-rum	{-um / Ĭ-um}	Ŭ-um	Ē-rum

The *Stem* is that part of the word which remains after the changeable endings are taken away.

The *Stems* of Nouns can be ascertained by taking away the terminations *um* or *rum* of the Genitive Plural. Hence the final letter of the Stem is in—

I.	II.	III.	IV.	V.
A	O	consonant or I	U	E

IV.—THE FIRST OR A DECLENSION.

The Nominative Singular of Nouns of the First Declension ends in ă.

	Sing.			Plur.	
Nom.	Mens-ă (*fem.*)	*a table*	Mens-ae,	*tables*	
Voc.	Mens-ă,	*O table*	Mens-ae,	*O tables*	
Acc.	Mens-am,	*a table*	Mens-ās,	*tables*	
Gen.	Mens-ae,	*of a table*	Mens-ārum,	*of tables*	
Dat.	Mens-ae,	*to* or *for a table*	Mens-Is,	*to* or *for tables*	
Abl.	Mens-ā,	*by, with,* or *from a table*	Mens-Is,	*by, with,* or *from tables*	

GENDER.—All Nouns of the First Declension are Feminine, unless they designate males: as, naută, *a sailor*.

V.—The Second or O Declension.

The Nominative Singular of Masculine Nouns of the Second Declension ends in ŭs and ĕr, and of Neuter Nouns in um.

A. Masculine.

1.

	Sing.			Plur.	
Nom.	Dŏmĭn-ŭs,	a lord	Dŏmĭn-ī,	lords
Voc.	Dŏmĭn-ĕ,	O lord	Dŏmĭn-ī,	O lords
Acc.	Dŏmĭn-um,	a lord	Dŏmĭn-ōs,	lords
Gen.	Dŏmĭn-ī,	of a lord	Dŏmĭn-ōrum,	of lords
Dat.	Dŏmĭn-ō,	to or for a lord	Dŏmĭn-īs,	to or for lords
Abl.	Dŏmĭn-ō,	by, with, or from a lord.	Dŏmĭn-īs,	by, with, or from lords.

2.

	Sing.			Plur.	
Nom.	Măgistĕr,	a master	Măgistr-ī,	masters
Voc.	Măgistĕr,	O master	Măgistr-ī,	O masters
Acc.	Măgistr-um,	a master	Măgistr-ōs,	masters
Gen.	Măgistr-ī,	of a master	Măgistr-ōrum,	of masters
Dat.	Măgistr-ō,	to or for a master	Măgistr-īs,	to or for masters
Abl.	Măgistr-ō,	by, with, or from a master.	Măgistr-īs,	by, with, or from masters.

3.

	Sing.			Plur.	
Nom.	Pŭĕr,	a boy	Pŭĕr-ī,	boys
Voc.	Pŭĕr,	O boy	Pŭĕr-ī,	O boys
Acc.	Pŭĕr-um,	a boy	Pŭĕr-ōs,	boys
Gen.	Pŭĕr-ī,	of a boy	Pŭĕr-ōrum,	of boys
Dat.	Pŭĕr-ō,	to or for a boy	Pŭĕr-īs,	to or for boys
Abl.	Pŭĕr-ō,	by, with, or from a boy.	Pŭĕr-īs,	by, with, or from boys.

B. Neuter.

	Sing.			Plur.	
N.V.A.	Rēgn-um,	a kingdom, or O kingdom	Rēgn-ă,	kingdoms, or O kingdoms
Gen.	Rēgn-ī,	of a kingdom	Rēgn-ōrum,	of kingdoms
Dat.	Rēgn-ō,	to or for a kingdom	Rēgn-īs,	to or for kingdoms
Abl.	Rēgn-ō,	by, with, or from a kingdom.	Rēgn-īs,	by, with, or from kingdoms.

NOTE.—The Nominative, Vocative, and Accusative of all Neuter Nouns are the same.

GENDER.—Most Nouns in ŭs are Masculine, but names of trees are Feminine; as, mālŭs, *an apple-tree.*

VI.—The Third or Consonant and I Declension.

The Nominative Singular of Nouns of the Third Declension ends in various letters. Their stems end in some consonant or i.

A. *Masculine and Feminine Nouns.*

I. Stem ending in a Consonant.

	Sing.		Plur.	
N.V.	Trăb-s (f.),	a beam, or O beam	Trăb-ĕs,	beams, or O beams
Acc.	Trăb-em,	a beam	Trăb-ĕs,	beams
Gen.	Trăb-ĭs,	of a beam	Trăb-um,	of beams
Dat.	Trăb-ī,	to or for a beam	Trăb-Ĭbŭs,	to or for beams
Abl.	Trăb-ĕ,	by, with, or from a beam.	Trăb-Ĭbŭs,	by, with, or from beams.

II. Stem ending in I.

	Sing.		Plur.	
N.V.	Host-ĭs (c.),	an enemy, or O	Host-ĕs,	enemies, or O enemies
Acc.	Host-em,	an enemy [enemy	Host-ĕs,	enemies
Gen.	Host-ĭs,	of an enemy	Host-Ĭum,	of enemies
Dat.	Host-ī,	to or for an enemy	Host-Ĭbŭs,	to or for enemies
Abl.	Host-ĕ,	by, with, or from an enemy.	Host-Ĭbŭs,	by, with, or from enemies.

B. *Neuter Nouns.*

I. Stem ending in a Consonant.

	Sing.		Plur.	
N.V.A.	Ŏpŭs,	a work, or O work	Ŏpĕr-ă,	works, or O works
Gen.	Ŏpĕr-ĭs,	of a work	Ŏpĕr-um,	of works
Dat.	Ŏpĕr-ī,	to or for a work	Ŏpĕr-Ĭbŭs,	to or for works
Abl.	Ŏpĕr-ĕ,	by, with, or from a work.	Ŏpĕr-Ĭbŭs,	by, with, or from works.

II. Stem ending in I.

	Sing.		Plur.	
N.V.A.	Măr-ĕ,	the sea, or O sea	Măr-Ĭă,	seas, or O seas.
Gen.	Măr-ĭs,	of the sea	Măr-Ĭum,	of seas
Dat.	Măr-ī,	to or for the sea	Măr-Ĭbŭs,	to or for seas
Abl.	Măr-ī,	by, with, or from the sea.	Măr-Ĭbŭs,	by, with, or from seas.

VII.—THE FOURTH OR U DECLENSION.

The Nominative Singular of Masculine and Feminine Nouns of the Fourth Declension ends in ŭs, and of Neuter Nouns in u.

1.

Sing.		Plur.	
N.V. Grăd-ŭs (m.),	a step, or O step	Grăd-ūs,	steps, or O steps
Acc. Grăd-um,	a step	Grăd-ūs,	steps
Gen. Grăd-ūs,	of a step	Grăd-ŭum,	of steps
Dat. Grăd-ŭī,	to or for a step	Grăd-Ibŭs,	to or for steps
Abl. Grăd-ū,	by, with, or from a step.	Grăd-Ibŭs,	by, with, or from steps.

2.

N.V.A. Gĕn-u (n.),	a knee or O knee	Gĕn-ŭă,	knees, or O knees
Gen. Gĕn-ūs,	of a knee	Gĕn-ŭum,	of knees
Dat. Gĕn-ū,	to or for a knee	Gĕn-Ibŭs,	to or for knees
Abl. Gĕn-ū,	by, with, or from a knee.	Gĕn-Ibŭs,	by, with, or from knees.

NOTE.—Some Nouns of the Fourth Declension make the *Dat.* and *Abl. Pl.* in *-ŭbŭs*: as, ăc-ŭbŭs, from ăc-ŭs, *a needle*; port-ŭbŭs, from port-ŭs, *a harbour*, and others.

GENDER.—Most Nouns of the Fourth Declension in **ŭs** are Masculine, but a few are Feminine: as, mănŭs, *a hand*; dŏmŭs, *a house*.

VIII.—THE FIFTH OR E DECLENSION.

The Nominative Singular of Nouns of the Fifth Declension ends in ēs.

Sing.		Plur.	
N.V. Dĭ-ēs,	a day, or O day	Dĭ-ēs,	days, or O days
Acc. Dĭ-em,	a day	Dĭ-ēs,	days
Gen. Dĭ-ēī,	of a day	Dĭ-ērum,	of days
Dat. Dĭ-ēī,	to or for a day	Dĭ-ēbŭs,	to or for days
Abl. Dĭ-ē,	by, with, or from a day.	Dĭ-ēbŭs,	by, with, or from days.

GENDER.—All Nouns of the Fifth Declension are Feminine except dĭēs, which is either Masculine or Feminine in the Singular, and always Masculine in the Plural; and mĕrīdĭēs, *midday*, which is always Masculine.

IX.—Adjectives of the First and Second Declensions.

Adjectives in ŭs, ă, um, or ĕr, (ĕ)ră, (ĕ)rum, are declined in the Masculine and Neuter like Nouns of the Second Declension, and in the Feminine like Nouns of the First Declension: as, bŏnŭs, bŏnă, bŏnum, *good;* nĭgĕr, nigră, nigrum, *black;* tĕnĕr, tĕnĕră, tĕnĕrum, *tender.*

1.

	Sing.			Plur.		
	M.	F.	N.	M.	F.	N.
Nom.	Bŏn-ŭs	bŏn-ă	bŏn-um	Bŏn-ī	bŏn-ae	bŏn-ă
Voc.	Bŏn-ĕ	bŏn-ă	bŏn-um	Bŏn-ī	bŏn-ae	bŏn-ă
Acc.	Bŏn-um	bŏn-am	bŏn-um	Bŏn-ōs	bŏn-ās	bŏn-ă
Gen.	Bŏn-ī	bŏn-ae	bŏn-ī	Bŏn-ōrum	bŏn-ārum	bŏn-ōrum
Dat.	Bŏn-ō	bŏn-ae	bŏn-ō	Bŏn-īs	bŏn-īs	bŏn-īs
Abl.	Bŏn-ō	bŏn-ă	bŏn-ō	Bŏn-īs	bŏn-īs	bŏn-īs

Nĭgĕr is declined in the Masculine like Măgistĕr.

2.

	M.	F.	N.	M.	F.	N.
N.V.	Nĭg-ĕr	nigr-ă	nigr-um	Nigr-ī	nigr-ae	nigr-ă
Acc.	Nigr-um	nigr-am	nigr-um	Nigr-ōs	nigr-ās	nigr-ă
Gen.	Nigr-ī	nigr-ae	nigr-ī	Nigr-ōrum	nigr-ārum	nigr-ōrum
Dat.	Nigr-ō	nigr-ae	nigr-ō	Nigr-īs	nigr-īs	nigr-īs
Abl.	Nigr-ō	nigr-ă	nigr-ō	Nigr-īs	nigr-īs	nigr-īs

Tĕnĕr is declined in the Masculine like Puĕr.

3.

	M.	F.	N.	M.	F.	N.
N.V.	Tĕnĕr	tĕnĕr-ă	tĕnĕr-um	Tĕnĕr-ī	tĕnĕr-ae	tĕnĕr-ă
Acc.	Tĕnĕr-um	tĕnĕr-am	tĕnĕr-um	Tĕnĕr-ōs	tĕnĕr-ās	tĕnĕr-ă
Gen.	Tĕnĕr-ī	tĕnĕr-ae	tĕnĕr-ī	Tĕnĕr-ōrum	tĕnĕr-ārum	tĕnĕr-ōrum
Dat.	Tĕnĕr-ō	tĕnĕr-ae	tĕnĕr-ō	Tĕnĕr-īs	tĕnĕr-īs	tĕnĕr-īs
Abl.	Tĕnĕr-ō	tĕnĕr-ă	tĕnĕr-ō	Tĕnĕr-īs	tĕnĕr-īs	tĕnĕr-īs

The only Adjectives declined like tĕnĕr are the following:—

asper, ĕra, ĕrum, *rough* | prosper, ĕra, ĕrum, *prosperous*
lacer, ĕra, ĕrum, *torn* | līber, ĕra, ĕrum, *free*
miser, ĕra, ĕrum, *wretched.*

With all Adjectives in fer and ger: as—

lānĭger, ĕra, ĕrum, *wool-bearing* | ŏpĭfer, ĕra, ĕrum, *help-bringing.*

X.—Adjectives of the Third Declension.

I. Adjectives of Three Terminations end in ĕr, rĭs, rĕ, and are declined like Nouns of the Third Declension. They have three terminations in the Nominative and Vocative Singular only: as, ăcĕr, ăcrĭs, ăcrĕ, *sharp;* cĕlĕr, cĕlĕrĭs, cĕlĕrĕ, *swift.*

	Sing.			Plur.	
	M.	F.	N.	M. and F.	N.
N.V.	Ăcĕr	ăcrĭs	ăcrĕ	Ăcrēs	ăcrĭă
Acc.	Ăcrem	ăcrem	ăcrĕ	Ăcrēs	ăcrĭă
Gen.	Ăcrĭs	ăcrĭs	ăcrĭs	Ăcrĭum	ăcrĭum
Dat.	Ăcrī	ăcrī	ăcrī	Ăcrĭbŭs	ăcrĭbŭs
Abl.	Ăcrī	ăcrī	ăcrī	Ăcrĭbŭs	ăcrĭbŭs

II. Adjectives of Two Terminations are declined like Nouns of the Third Declension. They have two terminations in the Nominative, Vocative, and Accusative only. They include—

1. Adjectives ending in ĭs: as, tristĭs (*masc.* and *fem.*), tristĕ (*neut.*), *sad.*
2. Comparatives, ending in ĭŏr, ĭŭs: as, mĕlĭŏr (*masc.* and *fem.*), mĕlĭŭs (*neut.*), *better.*

1.

	Sing.		Plur.	
	M. and F.	N.	M. and F.	N.
N.V.	Trist-ĭs	trist-ĕ	Trist-ēs	trist-ĭă
Acc.	Trist-em	trist-ĕ	Trist-ēs	trist-ĭă
Gen.	Trist-ĭs	trist-ĭs	Trist-ĭum	trist-ĭum
Dat.	Trist-ī	trist-ī	Trist-ĭbŭs	trist-ĭbŭs
Abl.	Trist-ī	trist-ī	Trist-ĭbŭs	trist-ĭbŭs

2.

	M. and F.	N.	M. and F.	N.
N.V.	Mĕlĭŏr	mĕlĭŭs	Mĕlĭŏr-ēs	mĕlĭŏr-ă
Acc.	Mĕlĭŏr-em	mĕlĭŭs	Mĕlĭŏr-ēs	mĕlĭŏr-ă
Gen.	Mĕlĭŏr-ĭs	mĕlĭŏr-ĭs	Mĕlĭŏr-um	mĕlĭŏr-um
Dat.	Mĕlĭŏr-ī	mĕlĭŏr-ī	Mĕlĭŏr-ĭbŭs	mĕlĭŏr-ĭbŭs
Abl.	Mĕlĭŏr-ĕ or ī	mĕlĭŏr-ĕ or ī	Mĕlĭŏr-ĭbŭs	mĕlĭŏr-ĭbŭs

III. Adjectives of One Termination are of various endings and declined like Nouns of the Third Declension: as, fēlix, *fortunate.*

	Sing.		Plur.	
	M. and F.	N.	M. and F.	N.
N.V.	Fēlix	fēlix	Fēlĭc-ēs	fēlĭc-ĭă
Acc.	Fēlĭc-em	fēlix	Fēlĭc-ēs	fēlĭc-ĭă
Gen.	Fēlĭc-ĭs	fēlĭc-ĭs	Fēlĭc-ĭum	fēlĭc-ĭum
Dat.	Fēlĭc-ī	fēlĭc-ī	Fēlĭc-ĭbŭs	fēlĭc-ĭbŭs
Abl.	Fēlĭc-ī or ĕ	fēlĭc-ī or ĕ	Fēlĭc-ĭbŭs	fēlĭc-ĭbŭs

XI.—ADJECTIVES AND NOUNS DECLINED TOGETHER.

I. FEMININE ADJECTIVE DECLINED ALONG WITH FEMININE NOUN, BOTH OF FIRST DECLENSION.

Sing.

N.V.	Parvă mensă,	a small table, or O small table
Acc.	Parvam mensam,	a small table
Gen.	Parvae mensae,	of a small table
Dat.	Parvae mensae,	to or for a small table
Abl.	Parvā mensā,	by, with, or from a small table.

Plur.

N.V.	Parvae mensae,	small tables, or O small tables
Acc.	Parvās mensās,	small tables
Gen.	Parvārum mensārum,	of small tables
Dat.	Parvīs mensīs,	to or for small tables
Abl.	Parvīs mensīs,	by, with, or from small tables.

II. MASCULINE ADJECTIVES DECLINED ALONG WITH MASCULINE NOUNS, BOTH OF SECOND DECLENSION.

(A.)

Sing.

Nom.	Bŏnŭs dŏmĭnŭs,	a good lord
Voc.	Bŏnĕ dŏmĭnĕ,	O good lord
Acc.	Bŏnum dŏmĭnum,	a good lord
Gen.	Bŏnī dŏmĭnī,	of a good lord
Dat.	Bŏnō dŏmĭnō,	to or for a good lord
Abl.	Bŏnō dŏmĭnō,	by, with, or from a good lord.

Plur.

N.V.	Bŏnī dŏmĭnī,	good lords, or O good lords
Acc.	Bŏnōs dŏmĭnōs,	good lords
Gen.	Bŏnōrum dŏmĭnōrum,	of good lords
Dat.	Bŏnīs dŏmĭnīs,	to or for good lords
Abl.	Bŏnīs dŏmĭnīs,	by, with, or from good lords.

(B.)

Sing.

Nom.	Bŏnŭs pŭĕr,	a good boy
Voc.	Bŏnĕ pŭĕr,	O good boy
Acc.	Bŏnum pŭĕrum,	a good boy
Gen.	Bŏnī pŭĕrī,	of a good boy
Dat.	Bŏnō pŭĕrō,	to or for a good boy
Abl.	Bŏnō pŭĕrō,	by, with, or from a good boy.

Plur.

N.V.	Bŏnī pŭĕrī,	good boys, or O good boys
Acc.	Bŏnōs pŭĕrōs,	good boys
Gen.	Bŏnōrum pŭĕrōrum,	of good boys
Dat.	Bŏnīs pŭĕrīs,	to or for good boys
Abl.	Bŏnīs pŭĕrīs,	by, with, or from good boys.

ADJECTIVES AND NOUNS.

III. Neuter Adjective declined along with Neuter Noun, both of Second Declension.

(A.)

Sing.

N.V.A.	Magnum regnum,	a great kingdom, or O great kingdom
Gen.	Magnī regnī,	of a great kingdom
Dat.	Magnō regnō,	to or for a great kingdom
Abl.	Magnō regnō,	by, with, or from a great kingdom.

Plur.

N.V.A.	Magnă regnă,	great kingdoms, or O great kingdoms
Gen.	Magnōrum regnōrum,	of great kingdoms
Dat.	Magnīs regnīs,	to or for great kingdoms
Abl.	Magnīs regnīs,	by, with, or from great kingdoms.

IV. Nouns of Third Declension, and Adjectives of First and Second Declensions, declined together.

1. Magnus Dux,—a great leader.

	Sing.	Plur.
Nom.	Magnŭs dux	Magnī dŭcēs
Voc.	Magnĕ dux	Magnī dŭcēs
Acc.	Magnum dŭcem	Magnōs dŭcēs
Gen.	Magnī dŭcĭs	Magnōrum dŭcum
Dat.	Magnō dŭcī	Magnīs dŭcĭbŭs
Abl.	Magnō dŭcĕ	Magnīs dŭcĭbŭs.

2. Bŏnă Lex,—a good law.

N.V.	Bŏnă lex	Bŏnae lēgēs
Acc.	Bŏnam lēgem	Bŏnās lēgēs
Gen.	Bŏnae lēgĭs	Bŏnārum lēgum
Dat.	Bŏnae lēgī	Bŏnīs lēgĭbŭs
Abl.	Bŏnă lēgĕ	Bŏnīs lēgĭbŭs.

3. Răpĭdum Flūmĕn,—a rapid river.

N.V.A.	Răpĭdum flūmĕn	Răpĭdă flūmĭnă
Gen.	Răpĭdī flūmĭnĭs	Răpĭdōrum flūmĭnum
Dat.	Răpĭdō flūmĭnī	Răpĭdīs flūmĭnĭbŭs
Abl.	Răpĭdō flūmĭnĕ	Răpĭdīs flūmĭnĭbŭs.

V. ADJECTIVES OF THIRD DECLENSION, DECLINED WITH NOUNS OF FIRST, SECOND, AND THIRD DECLENSIONS.

1. Cĕlĕrĭs săgittă,—*a swift arrow.*

	Sing.	Plur.
N.V.	Cĕlĕrĭs săgittă	Cĕlĕrēs săgittae
Acc.	Cĕlĕrem săgittam	Cĕlĕrēs săgittas
Gen.	Cĕlĕrĭs săgittae	Cĕlĕrum săgittārum
Dat.	Cĕlĕrī săgittae	Cĕlĕrĭbŭs săgittīs
Abl.	Cĕlĕrī săgittă	Cĕlĕrĭbŭs săgittīs

2. Tristĕ Proelium,—*a sad battle.*

	Sing.	Plur.
N.A.V.	Tristĕ proelĭum	Tristĭă proelĭă
Gen.	Tristĭs proelĭī	Tristĭum proelĭōrum
Dat.	Tristī proelĭō	Tristĭbŭs proelĭīs
Abl.	Tristī proelĭō	Tristĭbŭs proelĭīs

3. Fēlix Hŏmo,*—*a happy man.*

	Sing.	Plur.
N.V.	Fēlix hŏmo	Fēlĭcēs hŏmĭnēs
Acc.	Fēlĭcem hŏmĭnem	Fēlĭcēs hŏmĭnēs
Gen.	Fēlĭcĭs hŏmĭnĭs	Fēlĭcĭum hŏmĭnum
Dat.	Fēlĭcī hŏmĭnī	Fēlĭcĭbŭs hŏmĭnĭbŭs
Abl.	Fēlĭcī *or* ĕ hŏmĭnĕ	Fēlĭcĭbŭs hŏmĭnĭbŭs

* NOTE.—Nouns the stems of which end in ŏn or ōn (ĭn) have simply o in the *Nom. Sing.*: as, lĕo, lĕōn-em, *a lion*; hŏmo, hŏmĭn-em, *a man.*

XII.—COMPARISON OF ADJECTIVES.

Adjectives have three Degrees of Comparison: Positive, Comparative, and Superlative: as,

Positive.	Comparative.	Superlative.
Altŭs, *high.*	Altĭŏr, *higher.*	Altissĭmŭs, { *highest, most high, or very high.* }

The Comparative is formed by adding *ĭŏr* and the Superlative by adding *issĭmŭs* to the Positive, after taking away the termination of the Genitive Singular: as,

Nom. Posit.	Gen.		Comp.	Sup.
Altŭs,	Alt-ī,	*high,*	Alt-ĭŏr,	Alt-issĭmŭs,
Lĕvĭs,	Lĕv-ĭs,	*light,*	Lĕv-ĭŏr,	Lĕv-issĭmŭs,
Fēlix,	Fēlĭc-ĭs,	*fortunate,*	Fēlĭc-ĭŏr,	Fēlĭc-issĭmŭs,
Prūdens,	Prūdent-ĭs,	*prudent,*	Prūdent-ĭŏr,	Prūdent-issĭmŭs.

COMPARISON OF ADJECTIVES.

The Comparative is declined on p. 8 (měl-ĭor). The Superlative is declined like bŏnus, bŏna, bŏnum.

EXCEPTIONS.—I. Adjectives ending in ĕr form the Superlative in rĭmŭs: as,

Posit.			Comp.	Sup.
Nom.	Gen.			
pulchĕr,	pulchr-ī,	*beautiful,*	pulchr-ĭor,	pulcher-rĭmŭs.
lībĕr,	lībĕr-ī,	*free,*	lībĕr-ĭor,	līber-rĭmŭs.
ācĕr,	ācr-ĭs,	*sharp,*	ācr-ĭor,	ācer-rĭmŭs.
cĕlĕr,	cĕlĕr-ĭs,	*swift,*	cĕlĕr-ĭor,	cĕler-rĭmŭs.

Also vĕtŭs (*Gen.* vĕtĕr-is), *old,* has a Superlative, vĕter-rĭmŭs.

II. The following six Adjectives ending in ĭlĭs form their Superlative in lĭmŭs:

Posit.		Comp.	Sup.
făcĭlĭs,	*easy,*	făcĭl-ĭor,	făcil-lĭmŭs.
diffĭcĭlĭs,	*difficult,*	diffĭcĭl-ĭor,	diffĭcil-lĭmŭs.
sĭmĭlĭs,	*like,*	sĭmĭl-ĭor,	sĭmil-lĭmŭs.
dissĭmĭlĭs,	*unlike,*	dissĭmĭl-ĭor,	dissĭmil-lĭmŭs.
grăcĭlĭs,	*thin,*	grăcĭl-ĭor,	grăcil-lĭmŭs.
hŭmĭlĭs,	*low,*	hŭmĭl-ĭor,	hŭmil-lĭmŭs.

IRREGULAR COMPARISON.

Posit.		Comp.	Sup.
bŏnus,	*good,*	mĕlĭor,	optĭmŭs.
mălus,	*bad,*	pējor,	pessĭmŭs.
magnus,	*great,*	mājor,	maxĭmŭs.
parvus,	*small,*	mĭnor,	mĭnĭmŭs.
multus,	*much,*	plūs (*see below*),	plūrĭmŭs.

Plūs, the comparative of multus, is declined as follows:—

	Singular. Neut. only.	Plural. Masc. and Fem.	Neut.
Nom. & Acc.	} Plūs	Plūrēs	Plūră
Gen.	Plūrĭs	Plūrĭum	Plūrĭum
Dat.	Plūrī	Plūrĭbŭs	Plūrĭbŭs
Abl.	Plūrĕ	Plūrĭbŭs	Plūrĭbŭs

XIII.—THE NUMERALS.

Cardinal Numerals denote number simply or absolutely: as, ūnŭs, *one;* dŭŏ, *two;* trēs, *three.*

Ordinal Numerals denote numbers regarded as forming parts of a series: as, prīmŭs, *first;* sĕcundŭs, or altĕr, *second.* They are declined regularly as adjectives.

ARABIC SYMBOLS.	ROMAN SYMBOLS.	CARDINALS.	ORDINALS.
1	I	ūnus	prīmus.
2	II	dŭŏ	sĕcundus *or* altĕr.
3	III	trēs	tertĭus.
4	IV	quattŭŏr (quātŭŏr)	quartus.
5	V	quinquĕ	quintus.
6	VI	sex	sextus.
7	VII	septem	septĭmus.
8	VIII	octŏ	octāvus.
9	IX	nŏvem	nōnus.
10	X	dĕcem	dĕcĭmus.
11	XI	undĕcim	undĕcĭmus.
12	XII	duŏdĕcim	duŏdĕcĭmus.
13	XIII	trĕdĕcim	tertĭus dĕcĭmus.
14	XIV	quattuordĕcim	quartus dĕcĭmus.
15	XV	quindĕcim	quintus dĕcĭmus.
16	XVI	sēdĕcim	sextus dĕcĭmus.
17	XVII	septemdĕcim	septĭmus dĕcĭmus.
18	XVIII	duŏdēvīgintī	duŏdēvīcēsĭmus.
19	XIX	undēvīgintī	undēvīcēsĭmus.
20	XX	vīgintī	vīcēsĭmus.
100	C	centum	centēsĭmus.
1000	M *or* CIᴐ	millĕ	millēsĭmus.

The Cardinal Numerals, except ūnŭs, dŭŏ, trēs, are not declined. Mille is declined only in the plural. Ūnŭs is declined like bŏnŭs, except that the Genitive Singular (M., F., and N.) is ūnīus, and the Dative Singular (M., F., and N.) is ūnī.

Dŭŏ, *two,* trēs, *three,* and millĭă, *thousands,* are declined as follows:—

	M.	F.	N.	M. and F.	N.	N.
Nom.	Dŭ-ŏ	dŭ-ae	dŭ-ŏ	Trēs	trĭă	Millĭă
Acc.	Dŭ-ŏs *or* dŭ-ŏ	dŭ-ās	dŭ-ŏ	Trēs *or* trīs	trĭă	Millĭă
Gen.	Dŭ-ōrum	dŭ-ārum	dŭ-ōrum	Trĭum	trĭum	Millĭum
Dat.	Dŭ-ōbŭs	dŭ-ābŭs	dŭ-ōbŭs	Trĭbŭs	trĭbŭs	Millĭbŭs
Abl.	Dŭ-ōbŭs	dŭ-ābŭs	dŭ-ōbŭs	Trĭbŭs	trĭbŭs	Millĭbŭs

XIV.—The Pronouns.

I. Personal Pronouns.

1. *Pronoun of the First Person.*

	Sing.			Plur.	
Nom.	Ĕgŏ,	I	Nōs,		we
Acc.	Mē,	me	Nōs,		us
Gen.	Mĕī,	of me	Nostrī or nostrum,		of us
Dat.	Mĭhī,	to or for me	Nōbīs,		to or for us
Abl.	Mē,	by, with, or from me.	Nōbīs,		by, with, or from us.

2. *Pronoun of the Second Person.*

	Sing.			Plur.	
N.V.	Tū,	thou	Vōs,		ye
Acc.	Tē,	thee	Vōs,		you
Gen.	Tŭī,	of thee	Vestrī or vestrum,		of you
Dat.	Tĭbī,	to or for thee	Vōbīs,		to or for you
Abl.	Tē,	by, with, or from thee.	Vōbīs,		by, with, or from you.

3. *Pronoun of the Third Person.*

For the Pronoun of the Third Person, *he, she, it,* ĭs, ĕă, ĭd, is usually employed. (See p. 16.)

II. Reflective Pronoun of the Third Person.

The Reflective Pronoun refers to the Subject of the sentence, and cannot therefore have a Nominative case.

Sing. and Plur.

Acc.	Sē or sēsē,	*himself, herself, itself,* or *themselves.*
Gen.	Suī,	*of himself, herself, itself,* or *themselves.*
Dat.	Sĭbī,	*to* or *for himself, herself, itself,* or *themselves.*
Abl.	Sē or sēsē,	*by* or *from himself, herself, itself,* or *themselves.*

There are no distinct reflective forms in the 1st and 2nd persons; the different cases of *ego* and *tu* being used reflectively: as meī, *of myself;* tĭbi, *to thyself,* etc.

III. POSSESSIVE PRONOUNS.

These are formed from the First and Second Personal and the Third Reflective Pronouns, and are declined as adjectives:

M.	F.	N.	
Mĕus,	mĕa,	mĕum,	*my* or *mine*.
Tŭus,	tŭa,	tŭum,	*thy* or *thine*.
Noster,	nostra,	nostrum,	*our, ours*.
Vester,	vestra,	vestrum,	*your, yours*.
Sŭus,	sŭa,	sŭum,	*his, her, its, their*.

IV. DEMONSTRATIVE PRONOUNS.

1. Hic, haec, hoc, *this (near me)*; pl. *these*.

	Sing.			Plur.		
	M.	F.	N.	M.	F.	N.
Nom.	Hic	haec	hoc	Hī	hae	haec
Acc.	Hunc	hanc	hoc	Hōs	hās	haec
Gen.	Hūjus			Hōrum	hārum	hōrum
Dat.	Huic			His		
Abl.	Hōc	hāc	hōc	His		

2. Istĕ, istă, istŭd, *that (near you), that of yours*; pl. *those*.

Nom.	Istĕ	istă	istŭd	Istī	istae	istă
Acc.	Istum	istam	istŭd	Istōs	istās	istă
Gen.	Istīus			Istōrum	istārum	istōrum
Dat.	Istī			Istīs		
Abl.	Istō	istā	istō	Istīs		

3. Illĕ, illă, illŭd, *that, that yonder*; pl. *those*.

Nom.	Illĕ	illă	illŭd	Illī	illae	illă
Acc.	Illum	illam	illŭd	Illōs	illās	illă
Gen.	Illīus			Illōrum	illārum	illōrum
Dat.	Illī			Illīs		
Abl.	Illō	illā	illō	Illīs		

V. Determinate, Relative, and Interrogative Pronouns.

1. Ĭs, ĕă, ĭd, *he, she, it, that,* referring to the former part of a sentence.

	Sing.			Plur.	
	M.	F.	N.	M.	F.	N.
Nom.	Ĭs	ĕă	ĭd	Iī	eae	ĕă
Acc.	Eum	eam	ĭd	Eŏs	eās	ĕă
Gen.	Ējus			Eōrum	eārum	eōrum
Dat.	Eī			Iīs or eīs		
Abl.	Eŏ	eā	eŏ	Iīs or eīs		

2. Īdem, eădem, ĭdem, *the same.*

Nom.	Īdem	eădem	ĭdem	Iīdem	eaedem	eădem
Acc.	Eundem	eandem	ĭdem	Eōsdem	eāsdem	eădem
Gen.	Ējusdem			Eōrundem	eārundem	eōrundem
Dat.	Eīdem			Iīsdem or eisdem		
Abl.	Eōdem	eādem	eōdem	Iīsdem or eisdem		

3. Ipsĕ, ipsă, ipsum, *self, himself, herself, itself.*

Nom.	Ipsĕ	ipsă	ipsum	Ipsī	ipsae	ipsă
Acc.	Ipsum	ipsam	ipsum	Ipsŏs	ipsās	ipsă
Gen.	Ipsīus			Ipsōrum	ipsārum	ipsōrum
Dat.	Ipsī			Ipsīs		
Abl.	Ipsŏ	ipsă	ipsŏ	Ipsīs		

4. Relative—Quī, quae, quŏd, *who* or *which.*

Nom.	Quī	quae	quŏd	Quī	quae	quae
Acc.	Quem	quam	quŏd	Quŏs	quās	quae
Gen.	Cūjus			Quōrum	quārum	quōrum
Dat.	Cui			Quībus or quīs		
Abl.	Quŏ	quā	quŏ	Quībus or quīs		

5. Interrogative—Quĭs or quī, quae, quĭd or quŏd, *who? which? what?*

Nom.	Quĭs or quī	quae	quĭd or quŏd	Quī	quae	quae
Acc.	Quem	quam	quĭd or quŏd	Quŏs	quās	quae
Gen.	Cūjus			Quōrum	quārum	quōrum
Dat.	Cui			Quībus or quīs		
Abl.	Quŏ	quā	quŏ	Quībus or quīs		

XV.—The Verb.

Latin Verbs have two Voices:
    I. Active.   II. Passive.

Verbs have two Parts:
    I. Finite.   II. Infinite.

I. The Verb Finite has Three Moods:
    (1.) The Indicative Mood.
    (2.) The Subjunctive Mood.
    (3.) The Imperative Mood.

II. The Verb Infinite consists of Verbal Nouns and Adjectives:
    (1.) The Infinitive, which is a Verbal Noun.
    (2.) The Participle, which is a Verbal Adjective.
    (3.) The Supine, } which are Verbal Nouns.
    (4.) The Gerund, }

Verbs have Six Tenses:
  I. Three expressing unfinished action:
        Present.
        Imperfect.
        Future Simple.

  II. Three expressing finished action:
        Perfect.
        Pluperfect.
        Future Perfect.

Obs. The Perfect has the meaning of both a Present-Perfect and of an Indefinite-Past: thus, ămāvī signifies, *I have loved*, and *I loved*.

Verbs have two Numbers, Singular and Plural, and three Persons in each number.

Latin Verbs are arranged in four Classes, called Conjugations, distinguished by the final letter of the Stem, which is seen in the Infinitive Active. The Stem of

			Infinitive.
I. The First Conjugation ends in	A:	..	as, ămā-rĕ, *to love*.
II. The Second „ „	E:	..	as, mŏnē-rĕ, *to advise*.
III. The Third „ „	a Consonant or U:		as, { rĕg-ĕrĕ, *to rule*. { lŭ-ĕrĕ, *to pay*.
IV. The Fourth „ „	I:	..	as, audī-rĕ, *to hear*.

The Present Indicative, the Perfect Indicative, the Present Infinitive, and the Supine are called the *Principal Parts* of the Verb; because it is necessary to know these in order to conjugate a Verb.

XVI.—The Verb Sum, *I am.*

The Verb Sum is used in Latin, as the Verb To Be is in English, either as a Verb, as Via est longa, *the way is long;* or as an Auxiliary Verb, in which case it *helps* to form some of the Tenses of other Verbs: as, Mŏnĭtus sum, *I have been advised.*

Sum, fŭi, fŭtŭrŭs, essĕ,—*to be.* Stem: ĕs-, fu-.

VERB FINITE.

INDICATIVE MOOD.

1. Present Tense.

Sing.	Sum,	*I am*	*Plur.*	Sŭmŭs,	*We are*
	Es,	*thou art*		Estĭs,	*ye are*
	Est,	*he is.*		Sunt,	*they are.*

2. Imperfect Tense.

Sing.	Ĕram,	*I was*	*Plur.*	Ĕrămŭs,	*We were*
	Ĕrās,	*thou wast*		Ĕrātĭs,	*ye were*
	Ĕrăt,	*he was.*		Ĕrant,	*they were.*

3. Future-Simple Tense.

Sing.	Ĕro,	*I shall be*	*Plur.*	Ĕrĭmŭs,	*We shall be*
	Ĕrĭs,	*thou wilt be*		Ĕrĭtĭs,	*ye will be*
	Ĕrĭt,	*he will be.*		Ĕrunt,	*they will be.*

4. Perfect Tense.

Sing.	Fŭi,	*I have been,* or *I was*	*Plur.*	Fŭĭmŭs,	*We have been,* or *we were*
	Fŭistī,	*thou hast been,* or *thou wast*		Fŭistĭs,	*ye have been,* or *ye were*
	Fŭĭt,	*he has been,* or *he was.*		Fŭērunt ⎫ or fŭērĕ ⎭	*they have been,* or *they were.*

5. Pluperfect Tense.

Sing.	Fŭĕram,	*I had been*	*Plur.*	Fŭĕrāmŭs,	*We had been*
	Fŭĕrās,	*thou hadst been*		Fŭĕrātĭs,	*ye had been*
	Fŭĕrăt,	*he had been.*		Fŭĕrant,	*they had been.*

6. Future-Perfect Tense.

Sing.	Fŭĕro,	*I shall have been*	*Plur.*	Fŭĕrĭmŭs,	*We shall have been*
	Fŭĕrĭs,	*thou wilt have been*		Fŭĕrĭtĭs,	*ye will have been*
	Fŭĕrĭt,	*he will have been.*		Fŭĕrint,	*they will have been.*

THE VERB SUM.

IMPERATIVE MOOD.

1. Present Tense.

| Sing. Ĕs, | Be thou. | Plur. Estĕ, | Be ye. |

2. Future Tense.

Sing. Estŏ, Thou shalt or must be. Plur. Estōtĕ, Ye shall or must be.
Estŏ, he shall or must be. Suntŏ, They shall or must be.

SUBJUNCTIVE MOOD.

1. Present Tense.

Sing. Sim, I may be Plur. Sīmŭs, We may be
Sīs, thou mayst be Sītĭs, ye may be
Sĭt, he may be. Sint, they may be.

Obs. The first and third Persons singular and plural of the Present Subjunctive are often used as Imperatives; as, sint cīvēs justī, *let the citizens be just.*

2. Imperfect Tense.

Sing. Essem or fŏrem, I might be Plur. Essēmŭs or fŏrēmŭs, We might be
Essēs or fŏrēs, thou mightst be Essētĭs or fŏrētĭs, Ye might be
Essĕt or fŏrĕt, he might be. Essent or fŏrent, they might be.

3. Perfect Tense.

Sing. Fŭĕrim, I may have been Plur. Fŭĕrīmŭs, We may have been
Fŭĕrĭs, thou mayst have been Fŭĕrītĭs, ye may have been
Fŭĕrĭt, he may have been Fŭĕrint, they may have been.

4. Pluperfect Tense.

Sing. Fuissem, I should have been Plur. Fuissēmŭs, We should have been
Fuissēs, thou wouldst have been Fuissētĭs, ye would have been
Fuissĕt, he would have been. Fuissent, they would have been.

VERB INFINITE.

Infinitive Present, and Imperfect, Essĕ, to be.
Infinitive Perfect, and Pluperfect, Fuissĕ, to have been.
Infinitive Future, Fŭtūrŭs essĕ, or fŏrĕ, to be about to be.
Participle Future, Fŭtūrŭs, -a, -um, about to be.

Obs. Fŭtūrŭs may be conjugated with all the tenses of sum: as, fŭtūrŭs sum, *I am about to be;* fŭtūrŭs ĕram, *I was about to be,* &c.

XVII.—First or A Conjugation.—Active Voice.

Ămo, ămāvī, ămātum, ămārĕ,—*to love.* Stem: ăma-.

VERB FINITE.

INDICATIVE MOOD.

1. Present Tense.

Sing. Ămo,	I love, or am loving	*Plur.* Ăm-āmŭs,	We love, or are loving
Ăm-ās,	thou lovest, or art loving	Ăm-ātĭs,	ye love, or are loving
Ăm-ăt,	he loves, or is loving.	Ăm-ant,	they love, or are loving.

2. Imperfect Tense.

Sing. Ăm-ăbam,	I was loving	*Plur.* Ăm-ăbāmŭs,	We were loving
Ăm-ăbās,	thou wast loving	Ăm-ăbātĭs,	ye were loving
Ăm-ăbăt,	he was loving.	Ăm-ăbant,	they were loving.

3. Future-Simple Tense.

Sing. Ăm-ăbo,	I shall love	*Plur.* Ăm-ăbĭmŭs,	We shall love
Ăm-ăbĭs,	thou wilt love	Ăm-ăbĭtĭs,	ye will love
Ăm-ăbĭt,	he will love.	Ăm-ăbunt,	they will love.

4. Perfect Tense.

Sing. Ăm-āvī,	I have loved, or I loved	*Plur.* Ăm-āvĭmŭs,	We have loved, or we loved
Ăm-āvistī,	thou hast loved, or thou lovedst	Ăm-āvistĭs,	ye have loved, or ye loved
Ăm-āvĭt,	he has loved, or he loved.	Ăm-āvērunt, or ăm-āvērĕ	they have loved, or they loved.

5. Pluperfect Tense.

Sing. Ăm-āvĕram,	I had loved	*Plur.* Ăm-āvĕrāmŭs,	We had loved
Ăm-āvĕrās,	thou hadst loved	Ăm-āvĕrātĭs,	ye had loved
Ăm-āvĕrăt,	he had loved.	Ăm-āvĕrant,	they had loved.

6. Future-Perfect Tense.

Sing. Ăm-āvĕro,	I shall	*Plur.* Ăm-āvĕrĭmŭs,	We shall
Ăm-āvĕrĭs,	thou wilt } have	Ăm-āvĕrĭtĭs,	ye will } have
Ăm-āvĕrĭt,	he will } loved.	Ăm-āvĕrint,	they will } loved.

IMPERATIVE MOOD.

Present Tense.

Sing. Ăm-ā,	Love thou.	*Plur.* Ăm-ātĕ,	Love ye.

Future Tense.

Sing. Ăm-āto,	Thou shalt or must love	*Plur.* Ăm-ātōtĕ,	Ye shall or must love
Ăm-āto,	he shall or must love.	Ăm-anto,	they shall or must love.

FIRST CONJUGATION.—ACTIVE VOICE.

SUBJUNCTIVE MOOD.*

1. PRESENT TENSE.

Sing.	Ăm-em,	I may love	Plur.	Ăm-ĕmŭs,	We may love
	Ăm-ĕs,	thou mayst love		Ăm-ĕtĭs,	ye may love
	Ăm-ĕt,	he may love.		Ăm-ent,	they may love.

2. IMPERFECT TENSE.

Sing.	Ăm-ārem,	I might love	Plur.	Ăm-ārēmŭs,	We might love
	Ăm-ārēs,	thou mightst love		Ăm-ārētĭs,	ye might love
	Ăm-ārĕt,	he might love.		Ăm-ārent,	they might love.

3. PERFECT TENSE.

S.	Ăm-āvĕrim,	I may ⎫		P.	Ăm-āvĕrimŭs,	We may ⎫	
	Ăm-āvĕrīs,	thou mayst ⎬ have			Ăm-āvĕritĭs,	ye may ⎬ have
	Ăm-āvĕrĭt,	he may ⎭ loved.			Ăm-āvĕrint,	they may ⎭ loved.

4. PLUPERFECT TENSE.

S.	Ăm-āvissem,	I should ⎫	have	P.	Ăm-āvissēmŭs,	We should ⎫	have
	Ăm-āvissēs,	thou wouldst ⎬	loved.		Ăm-āvissētĭs,	ye would ⎬	loved.
	Ăm-āvissĕt,	he would ⎭			Ăm-āvissent,	they would ⎭	

* The 1st and 3rd Persons of the Present Subjunctive are often used with a kind of Imperative sense: ămem, *let me love;* ămĕt, *let him love;* ămēmŭs, *let us love.*

VERB INFINITE.

INFINITIVES.

PRES. and IMP.	} Ăm-ārĕ,	to love.
PERF. and PLUP.	} Ăm-āvissĕ,	{ to have loved.
FUTURE.	{ Ăm-ātūrŭs essĕ,	{ to be about to love.

SUPINES.

| Ăm-ātum, | to love. |
| Ăm-ātū, | in loving, or to be loved. |

GERUND.

Gen.	Ăm-andĭ,	of loving
Dat.	Ăm-andō,	for loving
Acc.	Ăm-andum,	loving
Abl.	Ăm-andō,	by loving.

PARTICIPLES.

PRESENT. Ăm-ans, -antis, *loving.*
FUTURE. Ăm-ātūrŭs (ă, um), *about to love.*

Obs. Ămātūrŭs may be conjugated with all the tenses of sum: as, ămātūrus sum, *I am about to love;* ămātūrus ĕram, *I was about to love,* &c.

NOTE.—In all the Perfect Tenses *vi* and *ve* may be omitted before *s* and *r*: as,

ămāvistī	becomes	ămastī		ămāvĕro	becomes	ămāro
ămāvistĭs	,,	ămastĭs		ămāvĕram	,,	ămāram
ămāvērunt	,,	ămārunt		ămāvĕrim	,,	ămārim
but ămāvērĕ does not become ămārĕ, which would be confounded with the Present Infin.				ămāvissem	,,	ămassem
				ămāvissĕ	,,	ămassĕ

XVIII.—Second or E Conjugation.—Active Voice.

Mŏneo, mŏnuī, mŏnĭtum, mŏnērĕ,—*to advise*. Stem: mŏne-.

VERB FINITE.
INDICATIVE MOOD.
1. Present Tense.

S. Mŏn-eo,	I advise, or am advising	P. Mŏn-ēmŭs,	We advise, or are advising
Mŏn-ēs,	thou advisest, or art advising	Mŏn-ētĭs,	ye advise, or are advising
Mŏn-ĕt,	he advises, or is advising.	Mŏn-ent,	they advise, or are advising.

2. Imperfect Tense.

S. Mŏn-ēbam,	I was advising	P. Mŏn-ēbāmŭs,	We were advising
Mŏn-ēbās,	thou wast advising	Mŏn-ēbātĭs,	ye were advising
Mŏn-ēbăt,	he was advising.	Mŏn-ēbant,	they were advising.

3. Future-Simple Tense.

S. Mŏn-ēbo,	I shall advise	P. Mŏn-ēbĭmŭs,	We shall advise
Mŏn-ēbĭs,	thou wilt advise	Mŏn-ēbĭtĭs,	ye will advise
Mŏn-ēbĭt,	he will advise.	Mŏn-ēbunt,	they will advise.

4. Perfect Tense.

S. Mŏn-uī,	I have advised, or I advised	P. Mŏn-uĭmŭs,	We have advised, or we advised
Mŏn-uistī,	thou hast advised, or advisedst	Mŏn-uistĭs,	ye have advised, or ye advised
Mŏn-uĭt,	he has advised, or he advised.	Mŏn-uērunt, or -uērĕ,	they have advised, or they advised.

5. Pluperfect Tense.

S. Mŏn-uĕram,	I had advised	P. Mŏn-uĕrāmŭs,	We had advised
Mŏn-uĕrās,	thou hadst advised	Mŏn-uĕrātĭs,	ye had advised
Mŏn-uĕrăt,	he had advised.	Mŏn-uĕrant,	they had advised.

6. Future-Perfect Tense.

S. Mŏn-uĕro,	I shall } have advised	P. Mŏn-uĕrĭmŭs,	We shall } have advised
Mŏn-uĕrĭs,	thou wilt }	Mŏn-uĕrĭtĭs,	ye will }
Mŏn-uĕrĭt,	he will }	Mŏn-uĕrint,	they will }

IMPERATIVE MOOD.
Present Tense.

S. Mŏn-ē,	Advise thou.	P. Mŏn-ētĕ,	Advise ye.

Future Tense.

S. Mŏn-ēto,	Thou shalt or must advise	P. Mŏn-ētōtĕ,	Ye shall or must advise
Mŏn-ēto,	he shall or must advise.	Mŏn-ento,	they shall or must advise.

SECOND CONJUGATION.—ACTIVE VOICE.

SUBJUNCTIVE MOOD.

1. Present Tense.

S. Mŏn-eam, I may advise
  Mŏn-eās, thou mayst advise
  Mŏn-eăt, he may advise.

P. Mŏn-eāmŭs, We may advise
  Mŏn-eātĭs, ye may advise
  Mŏn-eant, they may advise.

2. Imperfect Tense.

S. Mŏn-ērem, I might advise
  Mŏn-ērēs, thou mightst advise
  Mŏn-ērĕt, he might advise.

P. Mŏn-ērēmŭs, We might advise
  Mŏn-ērētĭs, ye might advise
  Mŏn-ērent, they might advise.

3. Perfect Tense.

S. Mŏn-uĕrim, I may }
  Mŏn-uĕrĭs, thou mayst } have advised
  Mŏn-uĕrĭt, he may }

P. Mŏn-uĕrĭmŭs, We may }
  Mŏn-uĕrĭtĭs, ye may } have advised
  Mŏn-uĕrint, they may }

4. Pluperfect Tense.

S. Mŏn-uissem, I should }
  Mŏn-uissēs, thou wouldst } have advised
  Mŏn-uissĕt, he would }

P. Mŏn-uissēmŭs, We should }
  Mŏn-uissētĭs, ye would } have advised
  Mŏn-uissent, they would }

VERB INFINITE.

INFINITIVES.

Pres. and Imp. } Mŏn-ērĕ, to advise.
Perf. and Plup. } Mŏn-uissĕ, { to have advised.
Future. { Mŏn-Ĭtūrŭs essĕ, { to be about to advise.

SUPINES.

Mŏn-ĭtum, to advise.
Mŏn-ĭtū, in advising, or to be advised.

GERUND.

Gen. Mŏn-endī, of advising
Dat. Mŏn-endō, for advising
Acc. Mŏn-endum, advising
Abl. Mŏn-endō, by advising.

PARTICIPLES.

Present. Mŏn-ens, -entis, advising.
Future. Mŏn-ĭtūrŭs, (ă, um), about to advise.

Obs. Mŏnĭtūrŭs may be conjugated with all the tenses of sum: as, mŏnĭtūrŭs sum, *I am about to advise;* mŏnĭtūrŭs ĕram, *I was about to advise,* &c.

XIX.—Third or Consonant and U Conjugation.— Active Voice.

Rĕgo, rexi, rectum, rĕgĕrĕ,—*to rule.* Stem: rĕg-.

VERB FINITE.

INDICATIVE MOOD.

1. Present Tense.

S. Rĕg-o, *I rule, or am* } *ruling.*
   Rĕg-ĭs, *thou rulest, or art*
   Rĕg-ĭt, *he rules, or is*

P. Rĕg-ĭmŭs, *We rule, or are* } *ruling.*
   Rĕg-ĭtĭs, *ye rule, or are*
   Rĕg-unt, *they rule, or are*

2. Imperfect Tense.

S. Rĕg-ēbam, *I was ruling*
   Rĕg-ēbās, *thou wast ruling*
   Rĕg-ēbăt, *he was ruling.*

P. Rĕg-ēbāmŭs, *We were ruling*
   Rĕg-ēbātĭs, *ye were ruling*
   Rĕg-ēbant, *they were ruling.*

3. Future-Simple Tense.

S. Rĕg-am, *I shall rule*
   Rĕg-ēs, *thou wilt rule*
   Rĕg-ĕt, *he will rule.*

P. Rĕg-ēmŭs, *We shall rule*
   Rĕg-ētĭs, *ye will rule*
   Rĕg-ent, *they will rule.*

4. Perfect Tense.

S. Rex-ī, *I have ruled, or I ruled*
   Rex-istī, *thou hast ruled, or thou ruledst*
   Rex-ĭt, *he has ruled, or he ruled.*

P. Rex-ĭmŭs, *We have ruled, or we ruled*
   Rex-istĭs, *ye have ruled, or ye ruled*
   Rex-ērunt or rex-ērĕ, } *they have ruled, or they ruled.*

5. Pluperfect Tense.

S. Rex-ĕram, *I had ruled*
   Rex-ĕrās, *thou hadst ruled*
   Rex-ĕrăt, *he had ruled.*

P. Rex-ĕrāmŭs, *We had ruled*
   Rex-ĕrātĭs, *ye had ruled*
   Rex-ĕrant, *they had ruled.*

6. Future-Perfect Tense.

S. Rex-ĕro, *I shall have ruled*
   Rex-ĕrĭs, *thou wilt have ruled*
   Rex-ĕrĭt, *he will have ruled.*

P. Rex-ĕrĭmŭs, *We shall have ruled*
   Rex-ĕrĭtĭs, *ye will have ruled*
   Rex-ĕrint, *they will have ruled.*

IMPERATIVE MOOD.

Present Tense.

S. Rĕg-ĕ, *Rule thou.*   P. Rĕg-ĭtĕ, *Rule ye.*

Future Tense.

S. Rĕg-ĭto, *Thou shalt or must rule*
   Rĕg-ĭto, *he shall or must rule.*

P. Rĕg-ĭtōtĕ, *Ye shall or must rule*
   Rĕg-unto, *they shall or must rule.*

THIRD CONJUGATION.—ACTIVE VOICE.

SUBJUNCTIVE MOOD.

1. Present Tense.

S. Rĕg-am,	I may rule		P. Rĕg-āmŭs,	We may rule	
Rĕg-ās,	thou mayst rule		Rĕg-ātĭs,	ye may rule	
Rĕg-ăt,	he may rule.		Rĕg-ant,	they may rule.	

2. Imperfect Tense.

S. Rĕg-ĕrem,	I might rule	P. Rĕg-ĕrēmŭs,	We might rule
Rĕg-ĕrēs,	thou mightst rule	Rĕg-ĕrētĭs,	ye might rule
Rĕg-ĕrĕt,	he might rule.	Rĕg-ĕrent,	they might rule.

3. Perfect Tense.

S. Rex-ĕrim,	I may	} have ruled.	P. Rex-ĕrĭmŭs,	We may	} have ruled.
Rex-ĕrĭs,	thou mayst		Rex-ĕrĭtĭs,	ye may	
Rex-ĕrĭt,	he may		Rex-ĕrint,	they may	

4. Pluperfect Tense.

S. Rex-issem,	I should	} have ruled.	P. Rex-issēmŭs,	We should	} have ruled.
Rex-issēs,	thou wouldst		Rex-issētĭs,	ye would	
Rex-issĕt,	he would		Rex-issent,	they would	

VERB INFINITE.

INFINITIVES.

Pres. and Imp.	Rĕg-ĕrĕ,	to rule.
Perf. and Plup.	Rex-issĕ,	to have ruled.
Future.	Rec-tūrŭs essĕ,	to be about to rule.

SUPINES.

Rec-tum,	to rule
Rec-tū,	in ruling, or to be ruled.

GERUND.

Gen. Rĕg-endī,	of ruling
Dat. Rĕg-endō,	for ruling
Acc. Rĕg-endum,	ruling
Abl. Rĕg-endō,	by ruling.

PARTICIPLES.

Present. Rĕg-ens, -entis, ruling
Future. Rec-tūrŭs (ă, um), about to rule.

Obs. Rectūrŭs may be conjugated with all the tenses of sum: as, rectūrŭs sum, *I am about to rule*; rectūrŭs ĕram, *I was about to rule*, &c.

XX.—FOURTH OR I CONJUGATION.—ACTIVE VOICE.

Audio, audīvī, audītum, audīrĕ,—*to hear.* Stem : audi-.

VERB FINITE.

INDICATIVE MOOD.

1. PRESENT TENSE.

S. Aud-io,	*I hear,* or *am* ⎫	*P.* Aud-īmŭs,	*We hear,* or *are* ⎫
Aud-īs,	*thou hearest,* or *art* ⎬ *hearing.*	Aud-ītĭs,	*ye hear,* or *are* ⎬ *hearing.*
Aud-ĭt,	*he hears,* or *is* ⎭	Aud-iunt,	*they hear,* or *are* ⎭

2. IMPERFECT TENSE.

S. Aud-iēbam,	*I was hearing*	*P.* Aud-iēbāmŭs,	*We were hearing*
Aud-iēbās,	*thou wast hearing*	Aud-iēbātĭs,	*ye were hearing*
Aud-iēbăt,	*he was hearing.*	Aud-iēbant,	*they were hearing.*

3. FUTURE-SIMPLE TENSE.

S. Aud-iam,	*I shall hear*	*P.* Aud-iēmŭs,	*We shall hear*
Aud-iēs,	*thou wilt hear*	Aud-iētĭs,	*ye will hear*
Aud-iĕt,	*he will hear.*	Aud-ient,	*they will hear.*

4. PERFECT TENSE.

S. Aud-īvī,	*I have heard,* or *I heard*	*P.* Aud-īvĭmŭs,	*We have heard,* or *we heard*
Aud-īvistī,	*thou hast heard,* or *thou heardst*	Aud-īvistĭs,	*ye have heard,* or *ye heard*
Aud-īvĭt,	*he has heard,* or *he heard.*	Aud-īvērunt, or -īvērĕ,	*they have heard,* or *they heard.*

5. PLUPERFECT TENSE.

S. Aud-īvĕram,	*I had heard*	*P.* Aud-īvĕrāmŭs,	*We had heard*
Aud-īvĕrās,	*thou hadst heard*	Aud-īvĕrātĭs,	*ye had heard*
Aud-īvĕrăt,	*he had heard.*	Aud-īvĕrant,	*they had heard.*

6. FUTURE-PERFECT TENSE.

S. Aud-īvĕro,	*I shall* ⎫	*P.* Aud-īvĕrimŭs,	*We shall* ⎫
Aud-īvĕrĭs,	*thou wilt* ⎬ *have heard.*	Aud-īvĕritĭs,	*ye will* ⎬ *have heard.*
Aud-īvĕrĭt,	*he will* ⎭	Aud-īvĕrint,	*they will* ⎭

IMPERATIVE MOOD.

PRESENT TENSE.

S. Aud-ī,	*Hear thou.*	*P.* Aud-ītĕ,	*Hear ye.*

FUTURE TENSE.

S. Aud-īto,	*Thou shalt* or *must hear*	*P.* Aud-ītōtĕ,	*Ye shall* or *must hear*
Aud-īto,	*he shall* or *must hear.*	Aud-iunto,	*they shall* or *must hear.*

FOURTH CONJUGATION.—ACTIVE VOICE.

SUBJUNCTIVE MOOD.

1. Present Tense.

S. Aud-iam,	I may hear	P. Aud-iāmŭs,	We may hear
Aud-iās,	thou mayst hear	Aud-iātĭs,	ye may hear
Aud-iăt,	he may hear.	Aud-iant,	they may hear.

2. Imperfect Tense.

S. Aud-īrem,	I might hear	P. Aud-īrēmŭs,	We might hear
Aud-īrēs,	thou mightst hear	Aud-īrētĭs,	ye might hear
Aud-īrĕt,	he might hear.	Aud-īrent,	they might hear.

3. Perfect Tense.

S. Aud-īvĕrim,	I may } have heard.	P. Aud-īvĕrimus,	We may } have heard.
Aud-īvĕrĭs,	thou mayst }	Aud-īvĕritĭs,	ye may }
Aud-īvĕrĭt,	he may }	Aud-īvĕrint,	they may }

4. Pluperfect Tense.

S. Aud-īvissem,	I should } have heard.	P. Aud-īvissēmŭs,	We should } have heard.
Aud-īvissēs,	thou wouldst }	Aud-īvissētĭs,	ye would }
Aud-īvissĕt,	he would }	Aud-īvissent,	they would }

VERB INFINITE.

INFINITIVES.

Pres. and Imp.	Aud-īrĕ,	to hear.
Perf. and Plup.	Aud-īvissĕ,	{to have heard.
Future.	{Aud-ītūrŭs essĕ,	{to be about to hear.

SUPINES.

| Aud-ītum, | to hear. |
| Aud-ītū, | in hearing, or to be heard. |

GERUND.

Gen.	Aud-iendī,	of hearing
Dat.	Aud-iendō,	for hearing
Acc.	Aud-iendum,	hearing
Abl.	Aud-iendō,	by hearing.

PARTICIPLES.

| Present. | Aud-iens, -entis, hearing. |
| Future. | Aud-ītūrŭs (ă, um), about to hear. |

Obs. Audītūrŭs may be conjugated with all the tenses of sum: as, audītūrŭs sum, *I am about to hear*; audītūrŭs ĕram, *I was about to hear*, &c.

Note.—In all the Perfect Tenses *v* is frequently omitted before *e* and *i*. The two *ii* are often contracted into *i*: as,

audīvistī becomes	{audīistī or audistī	audīvĕram becomes	audīĕram
audīvistĭs	„	{audīistĭs or audistĭs	audīvĕrim	„	audīĕrim
audīvĭt	„	audīĭt	audīvissem	„	{audīissem or audissem
audīvĕrunt	„	audīĕrunt	audīvissĕ	„	{audīissĕ or audissĕ
audīvĕro	„	audīĕro			

PART II.

QUESTIONS ON THE GRAMMATICAL FORMS.

I.—The Alphabet (page 1).

1. Of how many letters does the Latin Alphabet consist?
2. Into what two classes are the letters divided? Name them.
3. Which are the Vowels?
4. What are the remaining letters called?
5. Name the Diphthongs:
    (1) Those which are in common use.
    (2) Those which occur in only a few words.
6. How are Syllables marked as long or short?

II.—Parts of Speech (page 1).

1. How many Parts of Speech are there in the Latin language? Name them.
2. Is there an Article in the Latin language?
3. What is the Latin for *table, a table,* and *the table?*

III.—Substantives or Nouns (page 3).

1. How are Nouns declined?
2. How many Numbers have Latin Nouns? Name them.
3. How many Cases? Name them.
4. How many Genders? Name them.
5. What Nouns are said to be of *Common* Gender?
6. How many Declensions are there in Latin?
7. How can you tell of what Declension a Noun is?
8. What are the endings of the Genitive Case, Singular and Plural, of each of the Five Declensions?
9. What is the *Stem* of a word?
10. How can the Stem of a Noun be ascertained?
11. What is the final letter of the Stem in each of the Five Declensions?

IV.—The First or A Declension (page 3).

1. Decline like **Mensă**:—
   - ălă, *a wing.*
   - cŏlumbă, *a dove.*
   - cŏlōnĭă, *a colony.*
   - cŏrōnă, *a crown.*
   - insŭlă, *an island.*
   - portă, *a gate.*

2. Which is the distinguishing letter of the First Declension?

3. In what letter does the Nominative Singular of the First Declension end?

4. What is the Nominative Plural of **ălă**, *a wing?*

5. What is the Genitive Singular and Plural of **cŏlumbă**, *a dove?*

6. What is the Dative Singular and Plural of **cŏlōnĭă**, *a colony?*

7. What is the Accusative Singular and Plural of **cŏrōnă**, *a crown?*

8. What is the Vocative Singular and Plural of **insŭlă**, *an island?*

9. What is the Ablative Singular and Plural of **portă**, *a gate?*

10. What is the usual Gender of Nouns of the First Declension?

11. What Nouns of the First Declension are Masculine?

12. Put into English:—
    1. cŏlumbă (*nom.*). 2. cŏlumbae (*nom.*). 3. ălae (*gen.*). 4. ălārum. 5. cŏrōnae (*dat.*). 6. cŏrōnīs (*dat.*). 7. insŭlam. 8. insŭlās. 9. cŏlōnĭă (*voc.*). 10. cŏlōnĭae (*voc.*). 11. ălă (*abl.*). 12. ălīs (*abl.*). 13. portae (four meanings). 14. portīs (two meanings).

13. Put into Latin:—
    1. of a crown. 2. of crowns. 3. to the wing. 4. to wings. 5. the gate (*acc.*). 6. the gates (*acc.*). 7. O dove! 8. O doves! 9. with a crown. 10. by an island. 11. with gates.

V.—The Second or O Declension.

1. Nouns declined like Dŏmĭnŭs (page 4).

1. Decline like **Dŏmĭnŭs**:—
   - ămīcŭs, *a friend.*
   - ăvŭs, *a grandfather.*
   - ĕquŭs, *a horse.*
   - hortŭs, *a garden.*
   - ĭnĭmīcŭs, *an enemy.*
   - servŭs, *a slave.*
   - fīlĭŭs, *a son.*

   Note.—Nouns in ĭŭs form the Voc. Sing. in ī: as, fīlĭŭs, *a son*; Voc. fīlī, *O son!*

2. Which is the distinguishing letter of the Second Declension?

3. What are the endings of the Nom. Sing. of Masculine Nouns of the Second Declension?

4. What is the Gen. Sing. of Nouns of the Second Declension?

5. What is the Voc. Sing. of Nouns of the Second Declension whose Nom. ends in **us**? What exception is there?

6. What is the Nom. Pl. of **ĭnĭmīcŭs**, *an enemy?*

7. What is the Gen. Sing. and Pl. of **hortŭs**, *a garden?*

8. What is the Dat. Sing. and Pl. of **ăvŭs**, *a grandfather?*

9. What is the Acc. Sing. and Pl. of **ĕquŭs**, *a horse?*

10. What is the Voc. Sing. and Pl. of **ămīcŭs**, *a friend?*

11. What is the Abl. Sing. and Pl. of **servus**, *a slave*?

12. Put into English:—
1. ămīcī (*gen.*). 2. ămīcōrum. 3. ĭnĭmīcō (*dat.*). 4. ĭnĭmīcīs (*dat.*). 5. hortum. 6. hortōs. 7. servĕ. 8. servī (*voc.*). 9. ăvō (*abl.*). 10. ĕquīs (*abl.*). 11. hortī (three meanings). 12. ămīcō (two meanings). 13. hortīs (two meanings).

13. Put into Latin:—
1. of the horse. 2. of horses. 3. to a slave. 4. to slaves. 5. the friend (*acc.*). 6. the friends (*acc.*). 7. O friend! 8. O enemies! 9. by a slave. 10. with a grandfather. 11. by enemies. 12. with friends.

2. Nouns declined like **Măgistĕr** and **Pŭĕr** (page 4).

1. Decline like **Măgistĕr**:—
ăgĕr, *a field.*
lībĕr, *a book.*
mĭnistĕr, *a servant.*

2. Decline like **Pŭĕr**:—
gĕnĕr, *a son-in-law.*
sŏcĕr, *a father-in-law.*

3. What is the difference between the Voc. Sing. of **dŏmĭnŭs** and **măgistĕr**?

4. What is the difference in the manner of declining **măgistĕr** and **pŭĕr**?

5. What is the Nom. Sing. and Pl. of **lībĕr**, *a book*, and **sŏcĕr**, *a father-in-law*?

6. What is the Gen. Sing. and Pl. of **ăgĕr**, *a field*, and **gĕnĕr**, *a son-in-law*?

7. What is the Dat. Sing. and Pl. of **lībĕr**, *a book*, and **sŏcĕr**, *a father-in-law*?

8. What is the Acc. Sing. and Pl. of **mĭnistĕr**, *a servant*, and **gĕnĕr**, *a son-in-law*?

9. What is the Voc. Sing. and Pl. of **ăgĕr**, *a field*, and **sŏcĕr**, *a father-in-law*?

10. What is the Abl. Sing. and Pl. of **lībĕr**, *a book*, and **gĕnĕr**, *a son-in-law*?

11. Put into English:—
1. mĭnistĕr (*voc.*). 2. ăgrō (*dat.*). 3. sŏcĕrō (*abl.*). 4. lībrum. 5. mĭnistrōs. 6. gĕnĕrōs. 7. gĕnĕrī (*voc.*). 8. gĕnĕrōrum. 9. sŏcĕrīs (*abl.*). 10. sŏcĕr (two meanings). 11. gĕnĕrī (three meanings). 12. lībrō (two meanings). 13. mĭnistrīs (two meanings).

12. Put into Latin:—
1. O field! 2. of sons-in-law. 3. to a father-in-law. 4. with a servant. 5. of books. 6. with books. 7. the sons-in-law (*acc.*). 8. O servants! 9. of fields. 10. of a father-in-law.

3. Nouns declined like **Regnum** (page 4).

1. Decline like **Regnum**:—
dōnum, *a gift.*
oppĭdum, *a town.*
praemĭum, *a reward.*
proelĭum, *a battle.*
scūtum, *a shield.*
templum, *a temple.*

2. How many Cases are alike in Neuter Nouns, in both numbers? Name them.

THIRD DECLENSION. 31

3. What is the ending of each of these three Cases, in the Plural?
4. What is the Acc. Sing. and Pl. of **proelĭum**, *a battle?*
5. What is the Gen. Sing. and Pl. of **dōnum**, *a gift?*
6. What is the Abl. Sing. and Pl. of **templum**, *a temple?*
7. What is the Nom. Sing. and Pl. of **praemĭum**, *a reward?*
8. What is the Dat. Sing. and Pl. of **scūtum**, *a shield?*
9. What is the Voc. Sing. and Pl. of **oppĭdum**, *a town?*
10. Put into English:—
  1. templō (*dat.*). 2. dōnă (*acc.*). 3. templum (*voc.*).
4. scūtōrum. 5. templă (*nom.*). 6. dōnīs (*abl.*). 7. oppĭdō (*abl.*). 8. praemĭă (*voc.*). 9. dōnī. 10. templum (*acc.*). 11. proeliīs (*dat.*). 12. scūtă (three meanings). 13. dōnō (two meanings). 14. oppĭdīs (two meanings).
11. Put into Latin:—
  1. of a battle. 2. with a shield. 3. O temples! 4. rewards (*acc.*). 5. to a gift. 6. of rewards. 7. from battles. 8. the gift (*acc.*). 9. to the temples. 10. O reward! 11. the shields (*nom.*).

VI.—THE THIRD OR CONSONANT AND I DECLENSION.

A.—MASCULINE AND FEMININE NOUNS.

1. *Nouns whose Stems end in a* Consonant (page 5).

1. What are the distinguishing letters of the Third Declension?
2. What is meant by the *Stem* of a word? (*See page* 3.)
3. How may the *Stem* of a Noun be ascertained? (*See page* 3.)

4. Decline like **Trab-s**:—

(1) Nouns the stems of which end in the labial (lip) letters, *p, b, m.*

  princep-s, gen. **princĭp-ĭs,** *a chief.*
  hĭem-s, „ **hĭĕm-ĭs,** *winter.*

(2) Nouns the stems of which end in the guttural (throat) letters, *c, g.* NOTE.—In the Nom. and Voc. Sing. *cs, gs* are contracted into *x.*

  dux, gen. **dŭc-ĭs,** *a leader.*
  rex, „ **rēg-ĭs,** *a king.*
  lex, „ **lēg-ĭs,** *a law.*
  jūdex, „ **jūdĭc-ĭs,** *a judge.*

(3) Nouns the stems of which end in the dental (teeth) letters, *t, d.* NOTE.—In the *Nom. Sing. t* and *d* are dropped before *s*: as,

  lăpĭ-s, gen. **lăpĭd-ĭs,** *a stone.*
  custō-s, „ **custōd-ĭs,** *a guardian.*
  mīlĕ-s, „ **mīlĭt-ĭs,** *a soldier.*
  obsĕ-s, „ **obsĭd-ĭs,** *a hostage.*

32   QUESTIONS ON THE GRAMMATICAL FORMS.

Name the Stem of each of the above Nouns.*

5. What is the ending of the Gen. Sing. of Nouns of the Third Declension?
6. What is the ending of the Gen. Pl. of Nouns of the Third Declension?
7. What is the Dat. Sing. and Pl. of hĭems, *winter?*
8. What is the Voc. Sing. and Pl. of dux, *a leader?*
9. What is the Gen. Sing. and Pl. of mīlĕs, *a soldier?*
10. What is the Nom. Sing. and Pl. of rex, *a king?*
11. What is the Abl. Sing. and Pl. of obsĕs, *a hostage?*
12. What is the Acc. Sing. and Pl. of jūdex, *a judge?*
13. Put into English :—
 1. rĕgĕ. 2. jŭdĭcĭbŭs (dat.). 3. custŏdēs (acc.). 4. mīlĭtem. 5. custŏdĭbŭs (abl.). 6. jŭdĭcĭs. 7. obsĭdī. 8. mīlĭtēs (voc.). 9. rĕgum. 10. dūcēs (nom.). 11. jūdex (voc.). 12. mīlĭtĭbus (two meanings). 13. custōs (two meanings). 14. jūdĭcēs (three meanings).

14. Put into Latin :—
 1. O judges! 2. of the hostages. 3. with a guardian. 4. the leader (acc.). 5. to the soldiers. 6. O king! 7. of the guardians. 8. by a judge. 9. the hostages (acc.). 10. with soldiers. 11. the guardians.

2. *Nouns whose Stems end in* I (page 5).

1. Decline like Hostĭs :—

aurĭs,	gen.	aur-ĭs,	*an ear.*
cīvĭs,	,,	cīv-ĭs,	*a citizen.*
classĭs,	,,	class-ĭs,	*a fleet.*
turrĭs,	,,	turr-ĭs,	*a tower.*
vallĭs,	,,	vall-ĭs,	*a valley.*
cănĭs,	,,	căn-ĭs,	*a dog.*

NOTE.—Cănĭs, *a dog*, has a *Gen. Pl.* căn-um (not căn-ĭum).

2. What is the Abl. Sing. and Pl. of cīvĭs, *a citizen?*
3. What is the Gen. Sing. and Pl. of vallĭs, *a valley?*
4. What is the Nom. Sing. and Pl. of aurĭs, *an ear?*
5. What is the Dat. Sing. and Pl. of cănĭs, *a dog?*
6. What is the Acc. Sing. and Pl. of classĭs, *a fleet?*
7. What is the Voc. Sing. and Pl. of turrĭs, *a tower?*

8. Put into English :—
 1. turrĭs (gen.). 2. cīvĭbŭs (dat.). 3. vallēs (voc.). 4. aurem. 5. turrĭbŭs (abl.). 6. cīvĭum. 7. cīvĭs (voc.). 8. classĕ. 9. cănēs (nom.). 10. turrēs (acc.). 11. cīvī. 12. cănĭbŭs (two meanings). 13. classĭs (three meanings). 14. cīvēs (three meanings).

9. Put into Latin :—
 1. a dog (acc.). 2. the

---

* The more exact declension, according to the Consonant *stem*, will be learnt in *Principia Latina*, Part I.

THIRD DECLENSION. 33

valleys (*nom.*). 3. O citizens! 4. to the fleet. 5. from a tower. 6. to the valleys. 7. of citizens. 8. the towers (*acc.*). 9. O valley! 10. with dogs. 11. of the citizen.

B.—Neuter Nouns.

1. *Stems ending in a* **Consonant** (page 5).

1. Decline like **ŏpŭs**:—

crūs,	gen.	crūr-ĭs,	*a leg.*
corpŭs,	,,	corpŏr-ĭs,	*a body.*
lĭtŭs,	,,	lītŏr-ĭs,	*a shore.*
dĕcŭs,	,,	dĕcŏr-ĭs,	*an ornament.*
sīdŭs,	,,	sīdĕr-ĭs,	*a star.*
căpŭt,	,,	căpĭt-ĭs,	*a head.*

2. What three Cases are alike in both numbers in Neuter Nouns?

3. What is the ending of each of these three Cases, in the Plural?

4. What is the Voc. Sing. and Pl. of **corpŭs**, *a body?*

5. What is the Dat. Sing. and Pl. of **lĭtŭs**, *a shore?*

6. What is the Abl. Sing. and Pl. of **căpŭt**, *a head?*

7. What is the Acc. Sing. and Pl. of **crūs**, *a leg?*

8. What is the Gen. Sing. and Pl. of **dĕcŭs**, *an ornament?*

9. What is the Acc. Sing. and Pl. of **sīdŭs**, *a star?*

10. Put into English:—
1. corpŭs (*acc.*). 2. crūrĭbŭs (*abl.*). 3. dĕcŏrĭs. 4. lĭtŭs (*voc.*). 5. sīdĕrĭbŭs (*dat.*). 6. corpŏră (*acc.*). 7. sīdĕrĕ. 8. crūrī. 9. căpŭt (*acc.*). 10. corpŏrum. 11. sīdĕră (*nom.*). 12. lītŏrĭbŭs (two meanings). 13. căpĭtă (three meanings). 14. dĕcŭs (three meanings).

11. Put into Latin:—

1. a shore (*acc.*). 2. of the stars. 3. to an ornament. 4. heads (*acc.*). 5. O star! 6. the legs (*nom.*). 7. to bodies. 8. of a body. 9. O shores! 10. with ornaments. 11. a leg (*acc.*). 12. with the head. 13. bodies (*acc.*).

2. *Stems ending in* **I** (page 5).

1. Decline like **Mărĕ**:—

mărĕ,	gen.	măr-ĭs,	*the sea.*
rētĕ,	,,	rēt-ĭs,	*a net.*

2. Decline:—

ănĭmăl,	gen.	ănĭmāl-ĭs,	*an animal.*

3. What is the ending of the Abl. Sing. of Nouns of the Third Declension whose Stems end in i?

4. What is the Voc. Sing. and Pl. of **rētĕ**, *a net?*

5. What is the Nom. Sing. and Pl. of **mărĕ**, *the sea?*

6. What is the Dat. Sing. and Pl. of **ănĭmăl**, *an animal*?
7. What is the Acc. Sing. and Pl. of **rētĕ**, *a net*?
8. What is the Abl. Sing. and Pl. of **ănĭmăl**, *an animal*?
9. What is the Gen. Sing. and Pl. of **mărĕ**, *the sea*?
10. Put into English:—
 1. mărī. 2. rētĭum. 3. mărĕ (*acc.*). 4. ănĭmālĭbŭs (*dat.*). 5. mărĭă (*voc.*). 6. rētĭs. 7. rētĭbŭs (*abl.*). 8. ănĭmăl (*acc.*). 9. mărĭă (*acc.*). 10. mărĭs (*nom.*). 12. mărĭbŭs (two meanings). 13. ănĭmālĭă (three meanings). 14. rētĕ (three meanings).
11. Put into Latin:—
 1. from seas. 2. the animals (*acc.*). 3. O sea! 4. with a net. 5. the sea (*acc.*). 6. to the nets. 7. of the animals. 8. of the sea. 9. the nets (*acc.*). 10. O seas! 11. to the net. 12. the animals (*nom.*).

VII.—The Fourth or U Declension (page 6).

1. Decline like **Grădŭs**:—

currŭs,	gen.	curr-ūs,	*a chariot.*
exercĭtŭs,	,,	exercĭt-ūs,	*an army.*
fĭcŭs,	,,	fĭc-ūs,	*a fig.*
măgistrātŭs,	,,	măgistrāt-ūs,	*a magistrate.*
mănŭs,	,,	măn-ūs,	*a hand.*

2. What is the distinguishing letter of the Fourth Declension?
3. What is the Abl. Sing. and Pl. of **măgistrātŭs**, *a magistrate*?
4. What is the Acc. Sing. and Pl. of **fĭcŭs**, *a fig*?
5. What is the Nom. Sing. and Pl. of **currŭs**, *a chariot*?
6. What is the Gen. Sing. and Pl. of **mănŭs**, *a hand*?
7. What is the Dat. Sing. and Pl. of **măgistrātŭs**, *a magistrate*?
8. What is the usual ending of the Dat. and Abl. Pl.? What other ending is there?
9. What is the ending of the Dat. and Abl. Pl. of **ăcŭs**, *a needle*, and **portŭs**, *a harbour*?
10. What is the Voc. Sing. Pl. of **exercĭtŭs**, *an army*?
11. Decline like **Gĕnu**:—
cornu, gen. corn-ūs, *a horn*.
12. How many Cases have the same ending in the Singular Number of Neuter Nouns of the Fourth Declension? Name them.
13. Put into English:—
 1. mănĭbŭs (*dat.*). 2. exercĭtŭs (*gen.*). 3. mănū. 4. cornu (*acc.*). 5. currŭs (*acc.*). 6. fĭcŭs (*gen.*). 7. exercĭtŭs (*nom.*). 8. grădĭbŭs (*abl.*). 9. măgistrātŭs (*voc.*). 10. currŭum. 11. măgistrātŭs (*voc.*). 12. cornŭă (*acc.*). 13. exercĭtĭbŭs (two meanings). 14. mănŭs (two meanings). 15. mănŭs (four meanings). 16. cornŭă (three meanings). 17. cornu (five meanings).

14. Put into Latin:—
1. of the army. 2. a fig (*nom.*). 3. with the hands. 4. a horn (*acc.*). 5. to the armies. 6. the chariot (*acc.*). 7. of magistrates. 8. O armies! 9. the horns (*nom.*). 10. to a chariot. 11. the hands (*acc.*). 12. with an army. 13. O hand! 14. to figs.

VIII.—THE FIFTH OR E DECLENSION (page 6).

1. Decline like **Diēs**:—
    rēs, gen. rĕī, *a thing.*

NOTE (1).—**Diēs** and **rēs** are the only Nouns of the Fifth Declension that have a complete Plural.

2. Decline:—

ăcĭēs,	gen.	ăcĭēī,	*a line-of-battle.*
effĭgĭēs,	,,	effĭgĭēī,	*a likeness.*
făcĭēs,	,,	făcĭēī,	*a countenance.*
spēs,	,,	spĕī,	*hope.*

NOTE (2).—**Ăcĭēs, effĭgĭēs, făcĭēs**, and **spēs** have only a Nom., Acc., and Voc. in the Plural.

3. Decline:—

fĭdēs,	gen.	fĭdĕī,	*faith.*
mĕrĭdĭēs,	,,	mĕrĭdĭēī,	*mid-day.*
sĕgnĭtĭēs,	,,	sĕgnĭtĭēī,	*slothfulness.*

NOTE (3).—**Fĭdēs, mĕrĭdĭēs**, and **sĕgnĭtĭēs** have no Plural.

4. What is the distinguishing letter of the Fifth Declension?
5. Of what gender are almost all Nouns of the Fifth Declension?
6. Are any Nouns of the Fifth Declension Masculine?
7. Of what gender is **dĭēs**, *a day*?
8. What is the Acc. Sing. and Pl. of **făcĭēs**, *a countenance*?
9. What is the Abl. Sing. and Pl. of **rēs**, *a thing*?
10. What is the Voc. Sing. and Pl. of **effĭgĭēs**, *a likeness*?
11. What is the Dat. Sing. of **ăcĭēs**, *a line-of-battle*?
12. What is the Nom. Sing. and Pl. of **spēs**, *hope*?
13. What is the Gen. Sing. and Pl. of **dĭēs**, *a day*?

14. Put into English:—
1. ăcĭem. 2. rēbŭs (*dat.*). 3. spē. 4. fĭdĕī (*gen.*). 5. effĭgĭēs (*nom. pl.*). 6. dĭēbŭs (*abl.*). 7. spēs (*voc. sing.*). 8. spēs (*acc. pl.*). 9. rērum. 10. effĭgĭēī (*dat.*). 11. făcĭēs (*voc. pl.*). 12. rēs (five meanings). 13. ăcĭēī (two meanings). 14. rēbŭs (two meanings).

15. Put into Latin:—
1. by faith. 2. O days! 3. mid-day (*acc.*). 4. of slothfulness. 5. from things. 6. to a countenance. 7. days (*acc.*). 8. a likeness (*acc.*). 9. hopes (*nom.*). 10. of things. 11. to days. 12. O slothfulness!

IX.—Adjectives of the First and Second Declensions.

1. Adjectives declined like Bŏnŭs (page 7).

1. Decline like **Bŏnŭs**:—
   albŭs, *white.*
   magnŭs, *great.*
   multŭs, *much.*
   parvŭs, *small.*
   tĭmĭdŭs, *timid.*
   mălŭs, *bad.*
2. How is the Masculine of Adjectives in **ŭs, ă, um** declined?
3. How is the Feminine of Adjectives in **ŭs, ă, um** declined?
4. How is the Neuter of Adjectives in **ŭs, ă, um** declined?

5. What is the Acc. Sing. and Pl. of **magnŭs,** *great?*
6. What is the Gen. Sing. and Pl. of **parvŭs,** *small?*
7. What is the Abl. Sing. and Pl. of **mălŭs,** *bad?*
8. What is the Nom. Sing. and Pl. of **tĭmĭdŭs,** *timid?*
9. What is the Dat. Sing. and Pl. of **albŭs,** *white?*
10. What is the Voc. Sing. and Pl. of **multŭs,** *much?*

2. Adjectives declined like Nĭgĕr and Tĕnĕr (page 7).

1. Decline like **Nĭgĕr,** *black*:—
   pulchĕr, *beautiful.*
   aegĕr, *sick.*
   nostĕr, *our.*
   săcĕr, *sacred.*
2. Decline like **Tĕnĕr,** *tender*:
   lībĕr, *free.*
   aspĕr, *rough.*
3. How is the Masculine of Adjectives in **ĕr, ră, rum,** and **ĕr, ĕră, ĕrum** declined?
4. How is the Feminine of Adjectives in **ĕr, ră, rum,** and **ĕr, ĕră, ĕrum** declined?

5. How is the Neuter of Adjectives in **ĕr, ră, rum,** and **ĕr, ĕră, ĕrum** declined?
6. What is the Dat. Sing. and Pl. of **pulchĕr,** *beautiful?*
7. What is the Voc. Sing. and Pl. of **aegĕr,** *sick?*
8. What is the Gen. Sing. and Pl. of **nostĕr,** *our?*
9. What is the Nom. Sing. and Pl. of **săcĕr,** *sacred?*
10. What is the Abl. Sing. and Pl. of **lībĕr,** *free?*
11. What is the Abl. Sing. and Pl. of **aspĕr,** *rough?*

X.—Adjectives of the Third Declension.

1. Adjectives of Three Terminations (page 8).

1. What are the endings of the Nominative Case Singular of Adjectives of Three Terminations of the Third Declension?
2. In what Cases have they three Terminations only?

3. Decline like **Ācĕr,** *sharp*:—
   cĕlĕr, *swift.*
4. What is the Nom. Sing. and Pl. of **ācĕr,** *sharp?*
5. What is the Voc. Sing. and Pl. of **cĕlĕr,** *swift?*

ADJECTIVES AND NOUNS.

2. Adjectives of Two Terminations (page 8).

1. How many kinds of Adjectives of Two Terminations are there? What are they?
2. In what Cases have they two terminations only?
3. Decline like **Tristĭs**, *sad*:—
   - dĕbĭlĭs, *feeble.*
   - fĭdēlĭs, *faithful.*
   - fortĭs, *strong.*
   - grăvĭs, *heavy.*
4. Decline like **Mĕlĭŏr**, *better*:—
   - măjŏr, *greater.*
   - mĭnŏr, *less.*

5. What is the Dat. Sing. and Pl. of **dĕbĭlĭs**, *feeble?*
6. What is the Voc. Sing. and Pl. of **fĭdēlĭs**, *faithful?*
7. What is the Gen. Sing. and Pl. of **fortĭs**, *strong?*
8. What is the Acc. Sing. and Pl. of **grăvĭs**, *heavy?*
9. What is the Nom. Sing. and Pl. of **măjŏr**, *greater?*
10. What is the Abl. Sing. and Pl. of **mĭnŏr**, *less?*

3. Adjectives of One Termination (page 8).

1. Decline like **Fēlix**, *fortunate*:—
   - audax,   gen. audāc-ĭs,   *bold.*
   - răpax,   ,,   răpāc-ĭs,   *rapacious.*
   - vĕlox,   ,,   vĕlōc-ĭs,   *swift.*
   - dīvĕs,   ,,   dīvĭt-ĭs,   *rich.*
   - pŏtens,   ,,   pŏtent-ĭs,   *powerful.*
   - săpiens,   ,,   săpient-ĭs,   *wise.*

2. What is the Acc. Sing. and Pl. of **audax**, *bold?*
3. What is the Dat. Sing. and Pl. of **răpax**, *rapacious?*
4. What is the Abl. Sing. and Pl. of **vĕlox**, *swift?*

5. What is the Nom. Sing. and Pl. of **dīvĕs**, *rich?*
6. What is the Gen. Sing. and Pl. of **pŏtens**, *powerful?*
7. What is the Voc. Sing. and Pl. of **săpiens**, *wise?*

XI.—ADJECTIVES AND NOUNS DECLINED TOGETHER.

1. Feminine Adjectives declined along with Feminine Nouns, both of First Declension (page 9).

1. Decline like **Parvă Mensă**, *a small table*:—
   - magnă cŏrōnă,   *a great crown.*
   - tĭmĭdă cŏlumbă,   *the timid dove.*
   - pulchră pŭellă,   *a beautiful girl.*
   - lībĕră cŏlōnĭă,   *a free colony.*

2. What is the Gen. Sing. and Pl. of **magnă cŏrōnă**, *a great crown?*
3. What is the Nom. Sing. and Pl. of **tĭmĭdă cŏlumbă**, *the timid dove?*

4. What is the Dat. Sing. and Pl. of **pulchră pŭellă**, *a beautiful girl?*
5. What is the Acc. Sing. and Pl. of **lībĕră cŏlōnĭă**, *a free colony?*

QUESTIONS ON THE GRAMMATICAL FORMS.

6. What is the Abl. Sing. and Pl. of **magnă cŏrŏnă**, *a great crown?*

7. What is the Voc. Sing. and Pl. of **tĭmĭdă cŏlumbă**, *a timid dove?*

8. Put into English:—
 1. lībĕrīs cŏlōnĭīs (*abl.*). 2. tĭmĭdās cŏlumbās. 3. magnam cŏrōnam. 4. pulchrae pŭellae (*voc.*). 5. lībĕrae cŏlōnĭae (*dat.*). 6. tĭmĭdārum cŏlumbārum. 7. magnā cŏrōnā (*abl.*). 8. tĭmĭdae cŏlumbae (*gen.*). 9. pulchrā pŭellā (*voc.*). 10. lībĕrae cŏlōnĭae (*nom.*). 11. magnīs cŏrōnīs (*dat.*). 12. tĭmĭdīs cŏlumbīs (two meanings). 13. lībĕră cŏlōnĭă (two meanings). 14. magnae cŏrōnae (four meanings).

9. Put into Latin:—
 1. a timid dove (*acc.*). 2. beautiful girls (*nom.*). 3. by a free colony. 4. to a great crown. 5. O free colony! 6. great crowns (*acc.*). 7. of beautiful girls. 8. with great crowns. 9. O free colonies! 10. to the timid doves. 11. of free colonies.

2. MASCULINE ADJECTIVES DECLINED ALONG WITH MASCULINE NOUNS, BOTH OF SECOND DECLENSION.

A.—*With Nouns declined like* **Dŏmĭnŭs** (page 9).

1. Decline like **Bŏnŭs Dŏmĭnŭs**:—

tĭmĭdŭs servŭs,	*a timid slave.*
magnŭs hortŭs,	*a large garden.*
parvŭs ĕquŭs,	*a small horse.*
bĕnignŭs ăvŭs,	*a kind grandfather.*
doctŭs ămīcŭs,	*a learned friend.*
pĕrītŭs ĭnĭmīcŭs,	*a skilful enemy.*

2. What is the Abl. Sing. and Pl. of **parvŭs ĕquŭs**, *a small horse?*

3. What is the Acc. Sing. and Pl. of **bĕnignŭs ăvŭs**, *a kind grandfather?*

4. What is the Gen. Sing. and Pl. of **doctŭs ămīcŭs**, *a learned friend?*

5. What is the Voc. Sing. and Pl. of **magnŭs hortŭs**, *a large garden?*

6. What is the Dat. Sing. and Pl. of **pĕrītŭs ĭnĭmīcŭs**, *a skilful enemy?*

7. What is the Nom. Sing. and Pl. of **tĭmĭdŭs servŭs**, *a timid slave?*

8. Put into English:—
 1. Magnum hortum. 2. tĭmĭdōrum servōrum. 3. pĕrītī ĭnĭmīcī (*voc.*). 4. doctī ămīcī (*nom.*). 5. tĭmĭdō servō (*dat.*). 6. bĕnignōs ăvōs. 7. parvīs ĕquīs (*dat.*). 8. pĕrītō ĭnĭmīcō (*abl.*). 9. tĭmĭdīs servīs (*abl.*). 10. doctĕ ămīcĕ. 11. parvī ĕquī (*gen.*). 12. bĕnignō ăvō (two meanings). 13. doctīs ămīcīs (two meanings). 14. tĭmĭdī servī (three meanings).

9. Put into Latin:—
 1. learned friends (*acc.*).

ADJECTIVES AND NOUNS. 39

2. from a kind grandfather. 3. of a large garden. 4. O timid slave! 5. by skilful enemies. 6. to the learned friends. 7. O kind grandfathers! 8. of timid slaves. 9. the skilful enemy (*acc.*). 10. small horses (*nom.*). 11. to large gardens.

B.—*With Nouns declined like* **Pŭĕr** (page 9).

1. Decline like **Bŏnŭs Pŭĕr** :—
    bĕnignŭs sŏcĕr, *a kind father-in-law.*
    doctŭs gĕnĕr, *a learned son-in-law.*

2. What is the Acc. Sing. and Pl. of **bĕnignŭs sŏcĕr**, *a kind father-in-law*?
3. What is the Abl. Sing. and Pl. of **doctŭs gĕnĕr**, *a learned son-in-law*?
4. What is the Dat. Sing. and Pl. of **bĕnignŭs sŏcĕr**, *a kind father-in-law*?
5. What is the Voc. Sing. and Pl. of **doctŭs gĕnĕr**, *a learned son-in-law*?
6. What is the Nom. Sing. and Pl. of **bĕnignŭs sŏcĕr**, *a kind father-in-law*?
7. What is the Gen. Sing. and Pl. of **doctŭs gĕnĕr**, *a learned son-in-law*?
8. Put into English :—
    1. bĕnignīs gĕnĕrīs (*dat.*). 2. doctōs sŏcĕrōs. 3. bŏnī sŏcĕrī (*voc.*). 4. bĕnignō sŏcĕrō (*abl.*). 5. doctĕ gĕnĕr. 6. bĕnignōrum sŏcĕrōrum. 7. doctō gĕnĕrō (*dat.*). 8. bĕnignī gĕnĕrī (*gen.*). 9. bŏnum sŏcĕrum. 10. doctīs sŏcĕrīs (*abl.*). 11. bĕnignī gĕnĕrī (*nom.*). 12. bŏnō gĕnĕrō (two meanings). 13. bĕnignīs sŏcĕrīs (two meanings). 14. doctī gĕnĕrī (three meanings).

9. Put into Latin :—
    1. of the good sons-in-law. 2. O kind father-in-law! 3. a learned son-in-law (*acc.*). 4. good fathers-in-law (*acc.*). 5. to a learned father-in-law. 6. from good sons-in-law. 7. O kind fathers-in-law! 8. of a good father-in-law. 9. with a learned son-in-law. 10. good sons-in-law. 11. to the kind fathers-in-law.

3. NEUTER ADJECTIVES DECLINED ALONG WITH NEUTER NOUNS, BOTH OF SECOND DECLENSION (page 10).

1. Decline like **Magnum Regnum** :—
    parvum praemĭum, *a small reward.*
    aurĕum scūtum, *a golden shield.*
    magnum proelĭum, *a great battle.*
    antīquum templum, *an ancient temple.*
    pulchrum dōnum, *a beautiful gift.*
    injustum bellum, *an unjust war.*

2. What is the Voc. Sing. and Pl. of **aurĕum scūtum**, *a golden shield?*
3. What is the Gen. Sing. and Pl. of **antīquum templum**, *an ancient temple?*
4. What is the Dat. Sing. and Pl. of **injustum bellum**, *an unjust war?*
5. What is the Nom. Sing. and Pl. of **parvum praemĭum**, *a small reward?*
6. What is the Abl. Sing. and Pl. of **pulchrum dōnum**, *a beautiful gift?*
7. What is the Acc. Sing. and Pl. of **magnum proelĭum**, *a great battle?*
8. Put into English:—
  1. injustum bellum (*acc.*). 2. magnīs proeliīs (*dat.*). 3. pulchrǎ dōnǎ (*nom.*). 4. parvī praemiī. 5. antīquǎ templǎ (*voc.*). 6. aurĕŏ scūtŏ (*abl.*). 7. injustīs bellīs (*abl.*). 8. pulchrum dōnum (*voc.*). 9. antīquŏ templŏ (*dat.*). 10. parvǎ praemĭǎ (*acc.*). 11. aurĕōrum scūtōrum. 12. injustǎ bellǎ (three meanings). 13. magnum proelĭum (three meanings). 14. pulchrīs donīs (two meanings). 15. parvŏ praemĭŏ (two meanings).
9. Put into Latin:—
  1. O beautiful gifts! 2. to small rewards. 3. of an unjust war. 4. the ancient temples (*acc.*). 5. with golden shields. 6. a beautiful gift (*acc.*). 7. by a small reward. 8. of great battles. 9. golden shields (*nom.*). 10. O ancient temples! 11. to a great battle.

4. Nouns of Third Declension and Adjectives of First and Second Declensions declined together (page 10).

1. Decline like **Magnŭs Dux**:—
bŏnŭs rex, *a good king.*
injustŭs jūdex, *an unjust judge.*
2. What is the Abl. Sing. and Pl. of **bŏnŭs rex**, *a good king?*
3. What is the Nom. and Voc. Sing. and Pl. of **injustŭs jūdex,** *an unjust judge?*
4. What is the Gen. Sing. and Pl. of **bŏnŭs rex**, *a good king?*
5. What is the Dat. Sing. and Pl. of **injustŭs jūdex,** *an unjust judge?*
6. What is the Acc. Sing. and Pl. of **bŏnŭs rex**, *a good king?*
7. Put into English:—
  1. injustŏ rēgĕ. 2. bŏnī rēgēs (*nom.*). 3. injustī jūdĭcīs. 4. injustōs jūdĭcēs (*acc.*). 5. bŏnĕ rex. 6. injustōrum rēgum. 7. bŏnī jūdĭcēs (*voc.*). 8. bŏnīs rēgĭbŭs (*dat.*). 9. injustum jūdĭcem. 10. bŏnō rēgī. 11. injustīs jūdĭcĭbŭs. 12. injustī jūdĭcēs (two meanings). 13. bŏnīs jūdĭcĭbŭs (two meanings).
8. Put into Latin:—
  1. good kings (*acc.*). 2. of a good leader. 3. O unjust kings! 4. to the good judges. 5. by a good king. 6. a good leader (*acc.*). 7. of great kings. 8. good generals (*nom.*). 9. to an unjust king. 10. O unjust judge! 11. by good leaders.

ADJECTIVES AND NOUNS.

1. Decline like **Bŏnă Lex**:—
  magnă trabs, *a large beam.*
  nŏvă lex, *a new law.*

2. What is the Nom. and Voc. Sing. and Pl. of **nŏvă lex**, *a new law?*

3. What is the Dat. Sing. and Pl. of **magnă trabs**, *a large beam?*

4. What is the Acc. Sing. and Pl. of **magnă trabs**, *a large beam?*

5. What is the Abl. Sing. and Pl. of **nŏvă lex**, *a new law?*

6. What is the Gen. Sing. and Pl. of **nŏvă lex**, *a new law?*

7. Put into English:—
  1. nŏvae lēgī. 2. magnīs trăbĭbŭs (*abl.*). 3. nŏvās lēgēs. 4. magnă trabs (*voc.*). 5. magnae trăbĭs. 6. magnae trăbēs (*nom.*). 7. nŏvīs lēgĭbŭs (*dat.*). 8. magnă trăbĕ. 9. magnae trăbēs (*voc.*). 10. nŏvam lēgem. 11. magnārum trăbum. 12. nŏvīs trăbĭbŭs (two meanings). 13. nŏvae lēgēs (three meanings). 14. nŏvă lex (two meanings).

8. Put into Latin:—
  1. a new law (*acc.*). 2. to the good beams. 3. by new laws. 4. O great laws! 5. to a new beam. 6. of good beams. 7. by a great law. 8. of the good beam. 9. O new beam! 10. the great laws (*acc.*). 11. the good beams (*nom.*).

---

1. Decline like **Răpĭdum Flŭmĕn**:—
  bŏnum nōmĕn, *a good name.*
  săcrum carmĕn, *a sacred song.*

2. What is the Dat. and Abl. Sing. and Pl. of **bŏnum nōmĕn**, *a good name?*

3. What is the Nom., Acc., and Voc. Sing. and Pl. of **bŏnum nōmĕn**, *a good name?*

4. What is the Dat. and Abl. Sing. and Pl. of **săcrum carmĕn**, *a sacred song?*

5. What is the Nom., Acc., and Voc. Sing. and Pl. of **săcrum carmĕn**, *a sacred song?*

6. What is the Gen. Sing. and Pl. of **bŏnum nōmĕn**, *a good name?*

7. Put into English:—
  1. săcrī carmĭnĭs. 2. bŏnīs carmĭnĭbŭs (*abl.*). 3. săcrum nōmĕn (*acc.*). 4. săcrōrum carmĭnum. 5. săcră flŭmĭnă (*voc.*). 6. bŏnō carmĭnī. 7. săcrō nōmĭnĕ. 8. bŏnă carmĭnă (*acc.*). 9. săcrum flŭmĕn. 10. săcrīs nōmĭnĭbŭs (*dat.*). 11. săcră nōmĭnă (*nom.*). 12. bŏnum carmĕn (three meanings). 13. bŏnīs nōmĭnĭbŭs (two meanings). 14. săcră carmĭnă (three meanings.)

8. Put into Latin:—
  1. to a sacred name. 2. good songs (*nom.*). 3. by sacred rivers. 4. O sacred name! 5. to good songs. 6. a sacred river (*acc.*). 7. with a good song. 8. of sacred names. 9. the sacred rivers (*acc.*). 10. of a good song. 11. O sacred names!

5. ADJECTIVES OF THIRD DECLENSION WITH NOUNS OF FIRST, SECOND, AND THIRD DECLENSIONS (page 11).

1. Like Cĕlĕrĭs Săgittă.

1. Decline (in the Singular only):—
   ācrĭs Iră, *sharp (hasty and violent) anger.*

2. What is the Acc. Sing. of ācrĭs Iră, *sharp anger?*
3. What is the Abl. Sing. of ācrĭs Iră, *sharp anger?*
4. What is the Dat. Sing. of ācrĭs Iră, *sharp anger?*
5. What is the Gen. Sing. and Pl. of cĕlĕrĭs săgittă, *a swift arrow?*
6. What is the Dat. Sing. and Pl. of cĕlĕrĭs săgittă, *a swift arrow?*

2. Like Tristĕ Proelĭum.

1. Decline:—

   cīvīlĕ bellum,   *civil war.*
   tĕnŭĕ aurum,   *thin gold.*
   lĕvĕ scūtum,   *a light shield.*
   ūtĭlĕ dōnum,   *a useful gift.*
   mĕmŏrābĭlĕ templum,   *a memorable temple.*
   nōbĭlĕ praemĭum,   *a noble reward.*

2. What is the Voc. Sing. and Pl. of lĕvĕ scūtum, *a light shield?*
3. What is the Gen. Sing. and Pl. of ūtĭlĕ dōnum, *a useful gift?*
4. What is the Abl. Sing. of tĕnŭĕ aurum, *thin gold?*
5. What is the Nom. Sing. and Pl. of nōbĭlĕ praemĭum, *a noble reward?*
6. What is the Dat. Sing. and Pl. of cīvīlĕ bellum, *civil war?*
7. What is the Acc. Sing. and Pl. of mĕmŏrābĭlĕ templum, *a memorable temple?*
8. Put into English:—
   1. lĕvĭs scūtī. 2. tĕnŭĕ aurum (*acc.*). 3. nōbĭlĭă praemĭă (*acc.*). 4. lĕvĭbŭs scūtīs (*abl.*). 5. ūtĭlī dōnō (*abl.*). 6. mĕmŏrābĭlĭă templă (*voc.*). 7. ūtĭlĭbŭs dōnīs (*dat.*). 8. cīvīlĕ bellum (*voc.*). 9. mĕmŏrābĭlī templō (*dat.*). 10. cīvīlĭă bellă (*nom.*). 11. mĕmŏrābĭlĭum templōrum. 12. lĕvĕ scūtum (three meanings). 13. nōbĭlĭbŭs praemĭīs (two meanings). 14. lĕvĭă scūtă (three meanings).

9. Put into Latin:—
   1. useful gifts (*acc.*). 2. of light shields. 3. O memorable temple! 4. of thin gold. 5. O civil wars! 6. a useful gift (*acc.*). 7. of noble rewards. 8. from memorable temples. 9. light shields (*nom.*). 10. to a noble reward. 11. to memorable temples.

COMPARISON OF ADJECTIVES. 43

3. Like Fēlix Hŏmo.

1. Decline:—

ĭners virgo,	gen. ĭnert-ĭs virgĭn-ĭs,	*a sluggish maiden.*
audax mīlĕs,	„ audāc-ĭs mīlĭt-ĭs,	*a bold soldier.*
dīvĕs obsĕs,	„ dīvĭt-ĭs obsĭd-ĭs,	*a rich hostage.*
prūdens jūdex,	„ prūdent-ĭs jūdĭc-ĭs,	*a prudent judge.*
praestans lex,	„ praestant-ĭs lēg-ĭs,	*an excellent law.*
săpiens rex,	„ săpĭent-ĭs rēg-ĭs,	*a wise king.*

2. What is the Nom. Sing. and Pl. of **praestans lex**, *an excellent law*?

3. What is the Abl. Sing. and Pl. of **audax mīlĕs**, *a bold soldier*?

4. What is the Acc. Sing. and Pl. of **prūdens jūdex**, *a prudent judge*?

5. What is the Voc. Sing. and Pl. of **dīvĕs obsĕs**, *a rich hostage*?

6. What is the Gen. Sing. and Pl. of **săpiens rex**, *a wise king*?

7. What is the Dat. Sing. and Pl. of **ĭners virgo**, *a sluggish maiden*?

8. Put into English:—
   1. săpiens rex (*voc.*). 2. prūdentĭum jūdĭcum. 3. praestantēs lēgēs (*acc.*). 4. prūdentī jūdĭcī. 5. audācĭs mīlĭtĭs. 6. ĭnertĭbŭs virgĭnĭbŭs (*abl.*). 7. dīvĭtī or -ĕ obsĭdĕ. 8. audācēs mīlĭtēs (*voc.*). 9. săpĭentem rēgem. 10. dīvĭtēs obsĭdēs (*nom.*). 11. săpĭentĭbŭs rēgĭbŭs (*dat.*). 12. ĭnertēs virgĭnēs (three meanings). 13. audax mīlĕs (two meanings). 14. praestantĭbŭs lēgĭbŭs (two meanings).

9. Put into Latin:—
   1. to a sluggish maiden. 2. prudent maidens (*nom.*). 3. O prudent judge! 4. of an excellent law. 5. to a wise king. 6. rich hostages (*acc.*). 7. of prudent judges. 8. a bold soldier (*acc.*). 9. O sluggish maidens! 10. with bold soldiers. 11. from the sluggish maidens.

XII.—THE COMPARISON OF ADJECTIVES (pages 11, 12).

1. How many Degrees of Comparison are there? Name them.
2. How is the Comparative formed?
3. How is it declined?
4. How is the Superlative formed?
5. How is it declined?
6. Compare:—

altŭs,	*high.*
doctŭs,	*learned.*
lātŭs,	*wide.*
lĕvĭs,	*light.*
tristĭs,	*sad.*
fortĭs,	*strong.*
fēlix,	*fortunate.*
audax,	*bold.*
răpax,	*rapacious.*
prūdens,	*prudent.*
praestans,	*excellent.*
săpĭens,	*wise.*

7. How do Adjectives in ĕr form the Superlative?

8. Compare:—
pulchĕr, beautiful.
lībĕr, free.
ācĕr, sharp.
cĕlĕr, swift.

9. What is the Superlative of vĕtŭs, old?

10. How do Adjectives in ĭlĭs form their Superlative?

11. Compare:—
făcĭlĭs, easy.
diffĭcĭlĭs, difficult.

sĭmĭlĭs, like.
dissĭmĭlĭs, unlike.
grăcĭlĭs, thin.
hŭmĭlĭs, low.

12. Compare:—
bŏnŭs, good.
mălŭs, bad.
magnŭs, great.
parvŭs, small.
multŭs, much.

13. Of what is plūs the Comparative? Decline plūs.

XIII.—THE NUMERALS (page 13).

1. What do *Cardinal Numerals* denote?
2. What do *Ordinal Numerals* denote?
3. How are the *Ordinal Numerals* declined?
4. What are the Cardinal Numerals from 1 to 20, and of 100 and 1000?
5. What are the Ordinal Numerals from 1st to 20th, and of 100th and 1000th?
6. Decline ūnŭs, *one*. In what cases does it differ from bŏnŭs?
7. Decline dŭŏ, *two*.
8. Decline trēs, *three*.
9. Decline mīllĭă, *thousands*.
10. Put into English:—
1. dŭŏ hortī. 2. dŭae insŭlae. 3. dŭŏ regnă. 4. trĭum ămīcōrum. 5. dŭōbus ĕquīs (*dat.*). 6. dŭābus portīs (*abl.*). 7. quattŭŏr ămīcī. 8. quindĕcim servī. 9. octŏ rēgēs. 10. quinquĕ cŏlumbae. 11. centum custōdēs. 12. dŭŏdēvīgintī mīlĭtēs. 13. mīllĕ obsĭdēs. 14. dŭŏdĕcim mĭnistrī. 15. nŏvem oppĭdă. 16. quinquĕ templă.
11. Put into Latin:—
1. two horses. 2. two crowns. 3. three gifts. 4. of two doves. 5. by three gates. 6. seven hostages. 7. five kings. 8. eighteen gifts. 9. a thousand soldiers. 10. a hundred hostages. 11. nineteen slaves. 12. sixteen guardians. 13. eleven friends. 14. ten towns. 15. nine horses. 16. fourteen gates. 17. seventeen crowns.

12. Put into English:—
1. prīmŭs rex. 2. altĕră rēgīnă. 3. quintŭs mīlĕs. 4. dĕcĭmŭs jūdex. 5. octāvum dōnum. 6. vīcēsĭmŭs servŭs. 7. nōnŭs ăgĕr. 8. undĕcĭmă pŭella. 9. undēvīcēsĭmŭs hostĭs. 10. dŭŏdĕcĭmă cŏlōnĭă.

13. Put into Latin:—
1. the first friend. 2. the second gate. 3. the third king. 4. the sixth master. 5. the ninth queen. 6. the eleventh slave. 7. the twelfth garden. 8. the twentieth colony. 9. the eighth friend. 10. the tenth enemy.

XIV.—The Verb (page 17).

1. How many Voices have Latin Verbs?
2. Into what two parts are Verbs divided?
3. How many Moods has the Verb Finite? Name them.
4. Of what does the Verb Infinite consist?
5. How many Tenses have Verbs?
6. Into what two classes are these Tenses divided?
7. What are the Tenses in each of these classes?
8. What does **ămāvī** signify?
9. How many Numbers have Verbs, and how many Persons in each Number?
10. How are the four Conjugations distinguished?
11. Where is this distinction seen?
12. In what does the *Stem* of each of the Conjugations end? Give examples.
13. What are the *Principal Parts* of a Verb?
14. Why are they so called? Give an example.

XV.—The Verb **Sum**, *I am* (pages 18, 19).

1. How is the Verb **Sum** used in Latin?
2. What are the Principal Parts of the Verb **Sum**?

Indicative Mood.

The Present, Imperfect, and Future-Simple Tenses.

1. Conjugate the Present, Imperfect, and Future-Simple Tenses of the Indicative Mood of **Sum**.
2. What is the 3rd Pers. Sing. and Pl. of each of these Tenses of **Sum**?
3. What is the 1st Pers. Sing. and Pl.?
4. What is the 2nd Pers. Sing. and Pl.?
5. Put into English:—
   1. ĕrās. 2. ĕrĭmŭs. 3. ĕrāmŭs. 4. est. 5. ĕrātĭs. 6. ĕrĭtĭs. 7. sunt. 8. ĕro. 9. estĭs. 10. ĕrant. 11. ĕrunt. 12. sum. 13. ĕrĭs. 14. sŭmŭs. 15. ĕram. 16. ĕs. 17. ĕrĭt. 18. ĕrăt.
6. Put into Latin:—
   1. they were. 2. he will be. 3. thou art. 4. we shall be. 5. thou wast. 6. they are. 7. I am. 8. they will be. 9. ye were. 10. he is. 11. thou wilt be. 12. we were. 13. I shall be. 14. ye are. 15. he was. 16. ye will be. 17. we are. 18. I was.

The Perfect, Pluperfect, and Future-Perfect Tenses.

1. Conjugate the Perfect, Pluperfect, and Future-Perfect Tenses of the Indicative Mood of **Sum**.
2. What is the 2nd Pers. Sing. and Pl. of each of these Tenses of **Sum**?

3. What is the 1st Pers. Sing. and Pl.?

4. What is the 3rd Pers. Sing. and Pl.?

5. Put into English:—
1. fŭĕrĭt. 2. fŭĭmŭs. 3. fŭĕrās. 4. fŭistī. 5. fŭĕro. 6. fŭĕrint. 7. fŭĭt. 8. fŭĕram. 9. fŭistĭs. 10. fŭĕrĭs. 11. fŭĕrant. 12. fŭī. 13. fŭĕrăt. 14. fŭĕrĭtĭs. 15. fŭĕrĕ. 16. fŭĕrāmŭs. 17. fŭĕrunt. 18. fŭĕrimŭs. 19. fŭĕrātĭs.

6. Put into Latin:—
1. he had 2een. 2. we shall have been. 3. ye have been. 4. thou hadst been. 5. he has been. 6. I shall have been. 7. we had been. 8. thou hast been. 9. ye will have been. 10. they had been. 11. I have been. 12. thou wilt have been. 13. we have been. 14. they will have been. 15. I had been. 16. he will have been. 17. ye have been. 18. they had been.

XVI.—First or A Conjugation.—Active Voice
(pages 20, 21).

1. What is the distinguishing letter of the First Conjugation?
2. What are the Principal Parts of **ămo**, *I love*?
3. What are the Principal Parts of each of the following six verbs, conjugated like **ămo**?

laudo,	*I praise.*
ambŭlo,	*I walk.*
salto,	*I dance.*
vĭgĭlo,	*I watch.*
aedĭfĭco,	*I build.*
regno,	*I reign.*

Indicative Mood.
The Present, Imperfect, and Future-Simple Tenses.

1. Conjugate the Pres. Indic. of **ămo**, and of each of the six verbs named above.
2. Conjugate the Imperf. Indic. of **ămo**, and of each of the six verbs named above.
3. Conjugate the Fut.-Simp. Tense of **ămo**, and of each of the six verbs named above.
4. What is the 2nd Pers. Sing. and Pl. of the Imperf. Indic. of **aedĭfĭco**, *I build*?
5. What is the 1st Pers. Sing. and Pl. of the Fut.-Simp. of **ambŭlo**, *I walk*?
6. What is the 2nd Pers. Sing. and Pl. of the Pres. Indic. of **laudo**, *I praise*?
7. What is the 1st Pers. Sing. and Pl. of the Imperf. Indic. of **salto**, *I dance*?
8. What is the 3rd Pers. Sing. and Pl. of the Fut.-Simp. of **regno**, *I reign*?
9. What is the 3rd Pers. Sing. and Pl. of the Imperf. Indic. of **ambŭlo**, *I walk*?
10. What is the 1st Pers. Sing. and Pl. of the Pres. Indic. of **aedĭfĭco**, *I build*?
11. What is the 2nd Pers. Sing. and Pl. of the Fut.-Simp. of **laudo**, *I praise*?
12. What is the 3rd Pers. Sing. and Pl. of the Pres. Indic. of **salto**, *I dance*?
13. Put into English:—
1. ambŭlābĭs. 2. saltā-

VERBS.—FIRST CONJUGATION.

bant. 3. laudăt. 4. aedĭfĭcābămŭs. 5. laudăbĭt. 6. regnās. 7. ambŭlābunt. 8. saltābās. 9. vĭgĭlant. 10. regnābo. 11. ambŭlābātĭs. 12. saltăbĭt. 13. laudăbĭmŭs. 14. aedĭfĭcābăt. 15. regnāmŭs. 16. ambŭlābam. 17. vĭgĭlābĭtĭs. 18. saltātĭs.

14. Put into Latin:—
1. they were building. 2. he praises. 3. ye will dance. 4. we walk. 5. I shall praise. 6. he was watching. 7. they are dancing. 8. thou wilt build. 9. I was walking. 10. we shall reign. 11. thou art watching. 12. he will reign. 13. ye were dancing. 14. I praise. 15. they will build. 16. ye are walking. 17. we were building. 18. thou wast praising.

The Perfect, Pluperfect, and Future-Perfect Tenses.

1. Conjugate the Perf. Indic. of **ămo**, *I love*, and of each of the six verbs named above.
2. Conjugate the Pluperf. Indic. of **ămo**, and of each of the six verbs named above.
3. Conjugate the Fut.-Perf. of **ămo**, and of each of the six verbs named above.
4. What is the 2nd Pers. Sing. and Pl. of the Pluperf. Indic. of **ambŭlo**, *I walk*?
5. What is the 1st Pers. Sing. and Pl. of the Fut.-Perf. of **laudo**, *I praise*?
6. What is the 1st Pers. Sing. and Pl. of the Perf. Indic. of **aedĭfĭco**, *I build*?
7. What is the 3rd Pers. Sing. and Pl. of the Fut.-Perf. of **ambŭlo**, *I walk*?
8. What is the 3rd Pers. Sing. and Pl. of the Pluperf. Indic. of **salto**, *I dance*?
9. What is the 2nd Pers. Sing. and Pl. of the Perf. Indic. of **vĭgĭlo**, *I watch*?
10. What is the 2nd Pers. Sing. and Pl. of the Fut.-Perf. of **regno**, *I reign*?
11. What is the 1st Pers. Sing. and Pl. of the Pluperf. Indic. of **ambŭlo**, *I walk*?
12. What is the 3rd Pers. Sing. and Pl. of the Perf. Indic. of **laudo**, *I praise*?

13. Put into English:—
1. ambŭlāvĕrĭs. 2. saltāvĕrunt. 3. laudāvĕram. 4. vĭgĭlāvĕrĭmŭs. 5. aedĭfĭcāvĭt. 6. regnāvĕrăt. 7. saltāvĕrĭtĭs. 8. laudāvī. 9. ambŭlāvĕrant. 10. saltāvistī. 11. regnāvĕrĭt. 12. laudāvĕrātĭs. 13. ambŭlāvĭmŭs. 14. vĭgĭlāvĕro. 15. laudāvĕrāmŭs. 16. aedĭfĭcāvĕrint. 17. regnāvĕrĕ. 18. saltāvĕrās. 19. laudāvistĭs.

14. Put into Latin:—
1. he will have danced. 2. ye have watched. 3. thou hadst walked. 4. he reigned. 5. they will have walked. 6. I have praised. 7. ye had danced. 8. we shall have praised. 9. he has watched. 10. ye will have built. 11. they had

QUESTIONS ON THE GRAMMATICAL FORMS.

XVIII.—THIRD OR CONSONANT AND U CONJUGATION
(pages 24, 25).

1. What are the distinguishing letters of the 3rd Conjugation?
2. What are the Principal Parts of **rĕgo**, *I rule?*
3. Learn the Perfects and Supines of the following Verbs, conjugated like **rĕgo**, *I rule:*—

scrīb-o,	scrip-sī,	scrip-tum,	*I write.*
dūc-o,	duxī (duc-si),	duc-tum,	*I lead.*
ping-o,	pinxī (ping-si),	pic-tum,	*I paint.*
lūdo,	lūsī (lud-si),	lu-sum,	*I play.*
instrŭ-o,	instruxī,	instruc-tum,	*I arrange.*
vinc-o,	vic-ī,	vic-tum,	*I conquer.*

INDICATIVE MOOD.
The Present, Imperfect, and Future-Simple Tenses.

1. Conjugate the Pres. Indic. of **rĕgo**, *I rule*, and of each of the six verbs named above.
2. Conjugate the Imperf. Indic. of **rĕgo**, *I rule*, and of each of the six verbs named above.
3. Conjugate the Fut.-Simple of **rĕgo**, *I rule*, and of each of the six verbs named above.
4. What is the 2nd Pers. Sing. and Pl. of the Imperf. Indic. of **pingo**, *I paint?*
5. What is the 1st Pers. Sing. and Pl. of the Pres. Indic. of **lūdo**, *I play?*
6. What is the 3rd Pers. Sing. and Pl. of the Fut.-Simp. of **scrībo**, *I write?*
7. What is the 3rd Pers. Sing. and Pl. of the Pres. Indic. of **instrŭo**, *I arrange?*
8. What is the 2nd Pers. Sing. and Pl. of the Fut.-Simp. of **vinco**, *I conquer?*
9. What is the 1st Pers. Sing. and Pl. of the Imperf. Indic. of **dūco**, *I lead?*
10. What is the 2nd Pers. Sing. and Pl. of the Pres. Indic. of **scrībo**, *I write?*
11. What is the 3rd Pers. Sing. and Plur. of the Imperf. Indic. of **lūdo**, *I play?*
12. What is the 1st Pers. Sing. and Pl. of the Fut.-Simp. of **pingo**, *I paint?*

13. Put into English:—
   1. scrībĕtis. 2. lūdunt. 3. pingēbat. 4. dūcimŭs. 5. lūdĕt. 6. vincēbant. 7. pingis. 8. instrŭent. 9. scrībēbās. 10. instrŭēmŭs. 11. scrībo. 12. lūdēbātis. 13. lūdēs. 14. pingēbamŭs. 15. vincītis. 16. vincem. 17. dūcēbam. 18. pingĕt.

14. Put into Latin:—
   1. I was playing. 2. they are writing. 3. thou wilt paint. 4. they were writing. 5. I arrange. 6. he will conquer. 7. ye were leading. 8. we are conquering. 9. they will lead. 10. we were playing. 11. I shall arrange. 12. ye are playing. 13. we shall conquer. 14. he paints. 15. thou art playing. 16. he was arranging. 17. ye will play. 18. thou wast leading.

The Perfect, Pluperfect, and Future-Perfect Tenses.

1. Conjugate the Perf. Indic. of rĕgo, *I rule*, and of each of the six verbs named above.
2. Conjugate the Pluperf. Indic. of rĕgo, *I rule*, and of each of the six verbs named above.
3. Conjugate the Fut.-Perf. of rĕgo, *I rule*, and of each of the six verbs named above.
4. What is the 3rd Pers. Sing. and Pl. of the Perf. Indic. of pingo, *I paint?*
5. What is the 2nd Pers. Sing. and Pl. of the Fut.-Perf. of instrŭo, *I arrange?*
6. What is the 1st Pers. Sing. and Pl. of the Pluperf. Indic. of dūco, *I lead?*
7. What is the 3rd Pers. Sing. and Pl. of the Fut.-Perf. of scrībo, *I write?*
8. What is the 2nd Pers. Sing. and Pl. of the Perf. Indic. of vinco, *I conquer?*
9. What is the 3rd Pers. Sing. and Pl. of the Pluperf. Indic. of lūdo, *I play?*
10. What is the 1st Pers. Sing. and Pl. of the Perf. Indic. of dūco, *I lead?*
11. What is the 1st Pers. Sing. and Pl. of the Fut.-Perf. of vinco, *I conquer?*
12. What is the 2nd Pers. Sing. and Pl. of the Pluperf. Indic. of pingo, *I paint?*

13. Put into English:—
 1. instruxĕrās. 2. duxĕrunt. 3. pinxĕritĭs. 4. scripsĭt. 5. vicĕris. 6. lūdĕrātĭs. 7. pinxī. 8. instruxĕrant. 9. scripsĭmŭs. 10. duxĕrăt. 11. vicĕrint. 12. lūdistĭs. 13. scripsĕro. 14. duxĕrimŭs. 15. instruxĕram. 16. lūsĕrĭt. 17. duxĕrĕ. 18. vicĕrāmŭs. 19. instruxistī.

14. Put into Latin:—
 1. he led. 2. they had painted. 3. we have led. 4. I shall have arranged. 5. thou hadst played. 6. I conquered. 7. we had played. 8. thou hast written. 9. ye have painted. 10. they will have arranged. 11. I had written. 12. he will have led. 13. they conquered. 14. ye will have painted. 15. he has arranged. 16. ye had written. 17. thou wilt have played. 18. he had painted.

XIX.—FOURTH OR I CONJUGATION.—ACTIVE VOICE (pages 26, 27).

1. What is the distinguishing letter of the Fourth Conjugation?
2. What are the Principal Parts of audĭo, *I hear?*
3. What are the Principal Parts of the following verbs, conjugated like audĭo, *I hear?*
 dormĭo, *I sleep.*
 custōdĭo, *I guard.*
 pūnĭo, *I punish.*
 vestĭo, *I clothe.*
 fīnĭo, *I limit.*

4. Learn the Perfect and Supine of vĕnĭo, *I come,* conjugated like audĭo, *I hear:*—
 vĕnĭo, vĕni, ventum.

QUESTIONS ON THE GRAMMATICAL FORMS.

INDICATIVE MOOD.

The Present, Imperfect, and Future-Simple Tenses.

1. Conjugate the Pres. Indic. of **audĭo**, *I hear*, and of each of the six verbs named above.
2. Conjugate the Imperf. Indic. of **audĭo**, *I hear*, and of each of the six verbs named above.
3. Conjugate the Fut.-Simp. of **audĭo**, *I hear*, and of each of the six verbs named above.
4. What is the 3rd Pers. Sing. and Pl. of the Imperf. Indic. of **pūnĭo**, *I punish?*
5. What is the 2nd Pers. Sing. and Pl. of the Pres. Indic. of **vestĭo**, *I clothe?*
6. What is the 3rd Pers. Sing. and Pl. of the Fut.-Simp. of **fīnĭo**, *I limit?*
7. What is the 3rd Pers. Sing. and Pl. of the Pres. Indic. of **custōdĭo**, *I guard?*
8. What is the 1st Pers. Sing. and Pl. of the Imperf. Indic. of **dormĭo**, *I sleep?*
9. What is the 2nd Pers. Sing. and Pl. of the Fut.-Simp. of **vĕnĭo**, *I come?*
10. What is the 1st Pers. Sing. and Pl. of the Pres. Indic. of **pūnĭo**, *I punish?*
11. What is the 2nd Pers. Sing. and Pl. of the Imperf. Indic. of **fīnĭo**, *I limit?*
12. What is the 1st Pers. Sing. and Pl. of the Fut.-Simp. of **vestĭo**, *I clothe?*
13. Put into English:—
   1. vĕnĭĕt. 2. dormītĭs. 3. vĕnĭēbās. 4. vestĭt. 5. pūnĭēmŭs. 6. dormĭam. 7. vĕnĭēbam. 8. vestĭēbātĭs. 9. custōdĭĕs. 10. vestĭunt. 11. dormĭētĭs. 12. vĕnĭo. 13. custōdĭēbant. 14. dormīmŭs. 15. vestĭēbăt. 16. pūnĭent. 17. fīnĭs. 18. vĕnĭēbāmŭs.
14. Put into Latin:—
   1. they were sleeping. 2. ye will clothe. 3. he is coming. 4. he will punish. 5. thou wast guarding. 6. we limit. 7. I shall come. 8. ye were punishing. 9. thou art sleeping. 10. we shall limit. 11. he was coming. 12. they will clothe. 13. I was guarding. 14. they are coming. 15. I limit. 16. thou wilt sleep. 17. we were clothing. 18. ye are sleeping.

The Perfect, Pluperfect, and Future-Perfect Tenses.

1. Conjugate the Perf. Indic. of **audĭo**, *I hear*, and of each of the six verbs named above.
2. Conjugate the Pluperf. Indic. of **audĭo**, *I hear*, and of each of the six verbs named above.
3. Conjugate the Fut.-Perf. of **audĭo**, *I hear*, and of each of the six verbs named above.
4. What is the 2nd Pers. Sing. and Pl. of the Perf. Indic. of **vestĭo**, *I come?*
5. What is the 1st Pers. Sing. and Pl. of the Fut.-Perf. of **custōdĭo**, *I guard?*
6. What is the 3rd Pers. Sing. and Pl. of the Pluperf. Indic. of **pūnĭo**, *I punish?*
7. What is the 2nd Pers.

VERBS.—FOURTH CONJUGATION.

Sing. and Pl. of the Fut.-Perf. of **fīnĭo,** *I limit?*

8. What is the 1st Pers. Sing. and Pl. of the Perf. Indic. of **pŭnĭo,** *I punish?*

9. What is the 3rd Pers. Sing. and Pl. of the Fut.-Perf. of **custōdĭo,** *I guard?*

10. What is the 2nd Pers. Sing. and Pl. of the Pluperf. Indic. of **dormĭo,** *I sleep?*

11. What is the 1st Pers. Sing. and Pl. of the Pluperf. Indic. of **fīnĭo,** *I limit?*

12. What is the 3rd Pers. Sing. and Pl. of the Perf. Indic. of **vĕnĭo,** *I come?*

13. Put into English:—
1. vestīvĕrāmŭs. 2. dormīvĕrint. 3. fīnīvĭt. 4. custōdīvĕrĭs. 5. vestīvĭmŭs. 6. vĕnĕrĭt. 7. custōdīvĕram. 8. fīnīvĕrunt. 9. pŭnīvĕrĭtĭs. 10. custōdīvī. 11. vestīvĕrant. 12. vĕnĕrās. 13. dormīvĕrĭmŭs. 14. fīnīvĕrăt. 15. vestīvĭstĭs. 16. pŭnīvĕro. 17. fīnīvĭstī. 18. pŭnīvĕrātĭs. 19. custōdīvĕrĕ.

14. Put into Latin:—
1. thou hadst guarded. 2. he punished. 3. they had limited. 4. ye will have slept. 5. we have guarded. 6. I shall have come. 7. he had slept. 8. ye have limited. 9. he will have punished. 10. thou hast slept. 11. they will have guarded. 12. we had punished. 13. I have clothed. 14. thou wilt have come. 15. ye had limited. 16. they guarded. 17. we shall have punished. 18. I had come.

PART III.
EXERCISES.

Before beginning the Exercises two rules of Syntax must be learnt:—

RULE 1.—The Nominative Case denotes the SUBJECT. A Verb agrees with its Nominative case in number and person: as, pŭellă currĭt, *the girl runs;* pŭellae currunt, *the girls run.*

RULE 2.—The Accusative Case denotes the OBJECT. Transitive verbs govern an Accusative case: as, ăquĭlă ālās hăbĕt, *the eagle has wings.* NOTE.—In Latin the verb is put last and the Accusative case before it.

SOME RULES AS TO QUANTITY.

A vowel is either long by nature: as, māter, *a mother;* or long by position: as, mēnsa, *a table.*

(a) All diphthongs are long by nature: as, mensāē, *tables.*

(b) A vowel is long by position when it is followed by two or more consonants, or by a double consonant (x): as, mēnsa, *a table;* dūx, *a general.*

(c) A vowel before another vowel is usually short: as, pŭer, *a boy.*
  To this rule there are some exceptions, as in the Genitive and Dative Singular of the Fifth Declension: as, diēi; but rĕi and fidĕi obey the rule (see Vocabulary 9).

(d) *Us* as a final syllable is usually short: as, domĭnŭs, *a lord;* gradŭs, *a step.*
  To this rule there are also some exceptions; as in the Genitive Singular and Nominative, Accusative, and Vocative Plural of the Fourth Declension: as, manūs (see Exercises VIII., XX., and XXVI., and Vocabulary 8).

In words of more than two syllables the quantity of the last syllable but one is marked in these Exercises, when the following syllable begins with a consonant, as also in some other instances.

In words of two syllables the *accent* is on the first syllable. In words of three or more syllables the *accent* is on the last syllable but one, if this syllable is long; or on the last syllable but two, if the last syllable but one is short.

The First Declension.

Exercise I.
Nouns declined like **Mensa**.

Singular, 3 pers.
Cantăt, *(he, she, it) sings.*
Currĭt, *(he, she, it) runs.*

Plural, 3 pers.
Cantant, *(they) sing.*
Currunt, *(they) run.*

The Nouns and Verbs in this Exercise are the same as those in Exercises X. and XXII.

A.—1. Fīlia currit.
    2. Fīliae currunt.
    3. Fēmĭnae cantant.
    4. Fēmĭna cantat.
    5. Puellae currunt.
    6. Puella cantat.

    1. The woman runs.
    2. The women run.
    3. The girls sing.
    4. The daughter sings.
    5. The girl runs.
    6. The daughters sing.

Singular, 3 pers.
Hăbĕt, *(he, she, it) has.*

Plural, 3 pers.
Hăbent, *(they) have.*

B.—1. Regīna corōnam habet.
    2. Puella rosam habet.
    3. Fēmĭna fīliam habet.
    4. Colōnia columbas habet.
    5. Columbae alas habent.
    6. Insŭlae colonias habent.
    7. Puellae rosas habent.
    8. Colōnia insŭlas habet.
    9. Regīna filias habet.
  10. Insŭla columbas habet.

    1. The girl has a dove.
    2. The colony has women.
    3. The dove has wings.
    4. The island has colonies.
    5. The girls have doves.
    6. The women have roses.
    7. The colonies have islands.
    8. The queens have crowns.
    9. The islands have doves.
  10. The women have daughters.

The Second Declension.

Exercise II.

Nouns declined like **Dominus**.

The Nouns and Verbs in this Exercise are the same as those in Exercises XI. and XXIII.

A.—1. Servus currit.
2. Servi currunt.
3. Amīci cantant.
4. Amīcus currit.
5. Avus cantat.
6. Avi currunt.

1. The friend sings.
2. The friends run.
3. The slaves sing.
4. The grandfathers sing.
5. The slave sings.
6. The grandfather runs.

Singular, 3 pers.
Ămăt, (*he, she, it*) *loves.*

Plural, 3 pers.
Ămant, (*they*) *love.*

B.—1. Amīcus hortum amat.
2. Domĭnus servos habet.
3. Servi equos amant.
4. Inimīcus gladium habet.
5. Avus hortos habet.
6. Domĭni filios habent.
7. Equi fluvios amant.
8. Avi amīcos amant.
9. Servus equum amat.
10. Hortus fluvium habet.

1. The grandfather has a horse.
2. The friend loves the son.
3. The son has a grandfather.
4. The lord has sons.
5. The enemies have swords.
6. The friends have gardens.
7. The gardens have rivers.
8. The slaves love the lord.
9. The sons have grandfathers.
10. The friends have enemies.

The Second Declension.

Exercise III.

Nouns declined like **Magister** and **Puer**.

The Nouns and Verbs in this Exercise are the same as those in Exercises XII. and XXIV.

A.—1. Puer currit.
    2. Pueri currunt.
    3. Minister cantat.
    4. Gener currit.
    5. Soceri cantant.
    6. Ministri currunt.

    1. The servant runs.
    2. The servants sing.
    3. The boy sings.
    4. The father-in-law runs.
    5. The boys sing.
    6. The sons-in-law run.

B.—1. Magister ministrum habet.
    2. Socer puerum amat.
    3. Puer librum habet.
    4. Gener ministrum habet.
    5. Socer agrum habet.
    6. Magister libros habet.
    7. Soceri generos amant.
    8. Magistri ministros habent.
    9. Pueri agros amant.
    10. Magister pueros habet.

    1. The servant has a father-in-law.
    2. The son-in-law has boys.
    3. The master has a book.
    4. The boy loves the fields.
    5. The father-in-law has a son-in-law.
    6. The sons-in-law have fathers-in-law.
    7. The boys have books.
    8. The sons-in-law have servants.
    9. The boys love the field.
    10. The fathers-in-law have fields.

The Second Declension.

Exercise IV.

Nouns declined like **Regnum**.

The Nouns and Verbs in this Exercise are the same as those in Exercises XIII. and XXV.

Flŏrĕt, (*it*) *flourishes.*   Flŏrent, (*they*) *flourish.*
Mănĕt, (*it*) *remains.*   Mănent, (*they*) *remain.*

A.—1. Regnum manet.
    2. Oppĭda manent.
    3. Templa florent.
    4. Oppĭdum manet.
    5. Regna manent.
    6. Templum floret.

    1. The town flourishes.
    2. The temple remains.
    3. The kingdoms flourish.
    4. The temples remain.
    5. The kingdom flourishes.
    6. The towns flourish.

Ornăt, (*he, she, it*) *adorns.*   Ornant, (*they*) *adorn.*

B.—1. Oppĭdum templum habet.
    2. Templum aurum habet.
    3. Bellum praemia habet.
    4. Aurum templum ornat.
    5. Templa scuta habent.
    6. Proelia perīcŭlum habent.
    7. Bella proelia habent.
    8. Oppĭda dona habent.
    9. Regnum bella habet.
  10. Scuta templa ornant.

    1. The temple adorns the town.
    2. Gold adorns the shield.
    3. The town loves the gift.
    4. The kingdom has rewards.
    5. The temple has gifts.
    6. A battle has dangers.
    7. Gifts adorn the temple.
    8. The kingdoms have towns.
    9. The towns have temples.
  10. The temples have gold.

The Third Declension.

Exercise V.

Nouns declined like Trabs.

The Nouns and Verbs in this Exercise are the same as those in Exercises XIV. and XVII.

Pŭtăt, *(he, she, it) thinks.*   **Pŭtant,** *(they) think.*

A.—1. Judex putat.
2. Arx manet.
3. Custos currit.
4. Reges putant.
5. Trabes manent.
6. Milĭtes cantant.

1. The beam remains.
2. The king thinks.
3. The soldier sings.
4. The guardians run.
5. The citadels remain.
6. The judges think.

Cingĭt, *(he, she, it) surrounds.*   **Cingunt,** *(they) surround.*
Occĭdĭt, *(he, she, it) kills.*   **Occĭdunt,** *(they) kill.*

B.—1. Judex legem amat.
2. Rex urbem amat.
3. Dux milĭtes amat.
4. Arx custōdem habet.
5. Duces milĭtes habent.
6. Trabes duces occĭdunt.
7. Reges obsĭdes amant.
8. Custōdes judĭcem cingunt.
9. Urbes regem amant.
10. Milĭtes custōdes cingunt.

1. The beam kills the soldier.
2. The general has soldiers.
3. The soldier kills the hostage.
4. The hostages kill the general.
5. The citadel adorns the cities.
6. The kings have judges.
7. The laws have guardians.
8. Soldiers surround the king.
9. The guardians surround the citadel.
10. The king loves the cities.

Nouns of the Third Declension.

Exercise VI.

Nouns declined like **Hostis**.

The Nouns and Verbs in this Exercise are the same as those in Exercises XV. and XVIII.

A.—1. Vallis manet.
2. Canis currit.
3. Rupes manet.
4. Aves cantant.
5. Cives putant.
6. Turres manent.

1. The bird sings.
2. The tower remains.
3. The citizen thinks.
4. The rocks remain.
5. The dogs run.
6. The valleys remain.

B.—1. Civis hostem occīdit.
2. Vallis rupem cingit.
3. Canis civem amat.
4. Fames avem occīdit.
5. Hostes classem cingunt.
6. Rupes turrem cingunt.
7. Civis aves amat.
8. Canes aures habent.
9. Cives hostem cingunt.
10. Aves vallem amant.

1. The fleet surrounds the rock.
2. The dog kills the birds.
3. The bird has hunger.
4. The enemy has a fleet.
5. The rock has towers.
6. The citizens kill the dog.
7. Birds love the valleys.
8. The dogs love the citizens.
9. Valleys surround the rocks.
10. The valley has birds.

The Third Declension.

Exercise VII.

Neuter Nouns declined like **Opus** and **Mare**.

The Nouns and Verbs in this Exercise are the same as those in Exercises XVI. and XIX.

Cădĭt, *(he, she, it) falls.*   **Cădunt,** *(they) fall.*

A.—1. Decus cadit.
    2. Corpus manet.
    3. Anĭmal currit.
    4. Litŏra manent.
    5. Retia cadunt.
    6. Nomĭna manent.

    1. The shore remains.
    2. The net falls.
    3. The name remains.
    4. The animals run.
    5. The ornaments fall.
    6. The bodies remain.

B.—1. Rēte caput cingit.
    2. Mare lītus habet.
    3. Corpus caput habet.
    4. Decus nomen habet.
    5. Anĭmal crura habet.
    6. Sidĕra nomĭna habent.
    7. Decŏra litŏra cingunt.
    8. Animalia carmĭna amant.
    9. Litŏra mare cingunt.
  10. Retia gramen occĭdunt.

    1. Animals surround the shore.
    2. A net surrounds the animal.
    3. The shore surrounds the sea.
    4. The animal has a name.
    5. Grass surrounds the shore.
    6. Ornaments surround the head.
    7. Animals have heads.
    8. Nets surround the ornaments.
    9. Heads have bodies.
  10. Animals have legs.

The Fourth Declension.

Exercise VIII.
See Rule (d), page 54.

Nouns declined like **Gradus** and **Genu**.

The Nouns and Verbs in this Exercise are the same as those in Exercises XX. and XXVI.

Vĕnĭt, (he, she, it) comes.   **Vĕnĭunt,** (they) come.

A.—1. Lacus manet.
    2. Ficus cadit.
    3. Portus manet.
    4. Quercūs cadunt.
    5. Exercĭtūs vĕniunt.
    6. Magistrātūs putant.
    1. The army comes.
    2. The oak falls.
    3. The magistrate thinks.
    4. The harbours remain.
    5. The figs fall.
    6. The lakes remain.

Tĕnĕt, (he, she, it) holds.   **Tĕnent,** (they) hold.

B.—1. Exercĭtus equitātum habet.
    2. Cursus magistrātum occĭdit.
    3. Equitātus cursum amat.
    4. Lacus portūs habet.
    5. Manus acum tenet.
    6. Magistrātus currum habet.
    7. Quercūs lacūs ornant.
    8. Peditātus arcūs habet.
    9. Ficūs cornua cingunt.
  10. Manūs quercūs tenent.
    1. The cavalry surrounds the infantry.
    2. The magistrate has a chariot.
    3. The army surrounds the cavalry.
    4. Harbours surround the lake.
    5. The horn holds the figs.
    6. The hands hold the needles.
    7. Oaks surround the harbour.
    8. The magistrates have chariots.
    9. The armies have cavalry.
  10. Bows adorn the hands.

The Fifth Declension.

Exercise IX.

Nouns declined like **Dies.**

The Nouns and Verbs in this Exercise are the same as those in Exercises XXI. and XXVII.

A.—1. Facies manet.
    2. Dies vĕnit.
    3. Res manet.
    4. Effigies manent.
    5. Spes manent.
    6. Acies manent.

    1. The likeness remains.
    2. Hope comes.
    3. The line-of-battle remains.
    4. The things remain.
    5. The days come.
    6. The faces remain.

B.—1. Fides spem habet.
    2. Dies merīdĭem habet.
    3. Segnities diem occīdit.
    4. Facies effigiem habet.
    5. Acies planitiem cingit.
    6. Pernicies res cingit.
    7. Spes dies cingit.
    8. Facies spem habet.
    9. Dies planitiem ornat.
   10. Segnities spem occīdit.

    1. Hope surrounds the day.
    2. The day has hope.
    3. The plain has a line-of-battle.
    4. The things love the days.
    5. The days have a noon.
    6. Hope adorns things.
    7. The plain surrounds the line-of-battle.
    8. The noon adorns the days.
    9. The faces have hope.
   10. Hope kills slothfulness.

Adjectives of the First Declension.

Exercise X.

Nouns and Adjectives declined like **Mensa.**

Rule 3.—An Adjective agrees with its Noun in Gender, Number, and Case: as, servŭs tĭmĭdŭs, *a timid slave;* pŭellă tĭmĭdă, *a timid girl;* parvum oppĭdum, *a small town.*

Note that the Adjective in Latin is sometimes placed after the Noun. (See Exercises XIV. and XVII.)

The Nouns and Verbs in this Exercise are the same as those in Exercises I. and XXII.

A.—1. Bona filia currit.
2. Bonae filiae currunt.
3. Pulchrae femĭnae cantant.
4. Timĭda femĭna cantat.
5. Timĭdae puellae currunt.
6. Pulchra puella cantat.

1. The beautiful woman runs.
2. The timid women run.
3. The good girls sing.
4. The timid daughter sings.
5. The good girl runs.
6. The beautiful daughters sing.

B.—1. Bona regīna magnam corōnam habet.
2. Parva puella pulchram rosam habet.
3. Pulchra femĭna parvam filiam habet.
4. Magna colonia multas columbas habet.
5. Timĭdae columbae albas alas habent.
6. Parvae insŭlae magnas colonias habent.
7. Pulchrae puellae parvas rosas habent.
8. Libĕra colonia multas insŭlas habet.
9. Pulchra regīna pulchras filias habet.
10. Magna insŭla parvas columbas habet.

1. The beautiful girl has a little dove.
2. The free colony has many women.
3. The timid dove has beautiful wings.
4. The small island has many colonies.
5. The little girls have large doves.
6. The beautiful women have white roses.
7. The small colonies have beautiful islands.
8. The good queens have great crowns.
9. The large islands have timid doves.
10. The timid women have many daughters.

Adjectives of the Second Declension.

EXERCISE XI.

Nouns and Adjectives declined like **Dominus**.

The Nouns and Verbs in this Exercise are the same as those in Exercises II. and XXIII.

A.—1. Bonus servus currit.
2. Boni servi currunt.
3. Validi amici cantant.
4. Validus amicus currit.
5. Doctus avus cantat.
6. Docti avi currunt.

1. The learned friend sings.
2. The learned friends run.
3. The strong slaves sing.
4. The good grandfathers sing.
5. The strong slave sings.
6. The good grandfather runs.

B.—1. Bonus amicus magnum hortum amat.
2. Malus dominus timidos servos habet.
3. Boni servi parvos equos amant.
4. Validus inimicus bonum gladium habet.
5. Benignus avus magnos hortos habet.
6. Indocti domini validos filios habent.
7. Validi equi parvos fluvios amant.
8. Periti avi doctos amicos amant.
9. Parvus servus timidum equum amat.
10. Latus hortus magnum fluvium habet.

1. The kind grandfather has a good horse.
2. The learned friend loves the skilful son.
3. The skilful son has a learned grandfather.
4. The unlearned lord has strong sons.
5. The strong enemies have broad swords.
6. The learned friends have large gardens.
7. The large gardens have wide rivers.
8. The timid slaves love the kind lord.
9. The good sons have kind grandfathers.
10. The skilful friends have strong enemies.

Adjectives of the Second Declension.

Exercise XII.

Nouns and Adjectives declined like **Magister** and **Puer**.

The Nouns and Verbs in this Exercise are the same as those in Exercises III. and XXIV.

A.—1. Līber puer currit.
2. Libĕri puĕri currunt.
3. Aeger minister cantat.
4. Niger gener currit.
5. Aspĕri socĕri cantant.
6. Aegri ministri currunt.

1. The black servant runs.
2. The black servants sing.
3. The rough boy sings.
4. The free father-in-law runs.
5. The rough boys sing.
6. The sick sons-in-law run.

B.—1. Magister vester libĕrum ministrum habet.
2. Asper socer tenĕrum puĕrum amat.
3. Aeger puer librum vestrum habet.
4. Tener gener nigrum ministrum habet.
5. Socer vester libĕrum agrum habet.
6. Magister noster sacros libros habet.
7. Aegri socĕri tenĕros genĕros amant.
8. Magistri nostri libĕros ministros habent.
9. Aspĕri puĕri agros nostros amant.
10. Vester * magister aspĕros puĕros habet.

1. The black servant has a free father-in-law.
2. The rough son-in-law has tender boys.
3. *Our* master has *your* book.
4. The rough boy loves our fields.
5. The tender father-in-law has a rough son-in-law.
6. The rough sons-in-law have tender fathers-in-law.
7. The black boys have sacred books.
8. Your sons-in-law have black servants.
9. The sick boys love your field.
10. Our fathers-in-law have rough fields.

* The pronominal adjectives *noster* and *vester*, when placed immediately *before* a substantive, are emphatic.

Adjectives of the Second Declension.

Exercise XIII.

Nouns and Adjectives declined like **Regnum**.

The Nouns and Verbs in this Exercise are the same as those in Exercises IV. and XXV.

A.—1. Parvum regnum manet.
 2. Magna oppĭda manent.
 3. Pulchra templa florent.
 4. Magnum oppĭdum manet.
 5. Antīqua regna manent.
 6. Pulchrum templum floret.

 1. The beautiful town flourishes.
 2. The small temple remains.
 3. The large kingdoms flourish.
 4. The ancient temples remain.
 5. The large kingdom flourishes.
 6. The beautiful towns flourish.

B.—1. Antīquum oppĭdum magnum templum habet.
 2. Pulchrum templum multum aurum habet.
 3. Injustum bellum parva praemia habet.
 4. Multum aurum pulchrum templum ornat.
 5. Antīqua templa aurĕa scuta habent.
 6. Magna proelia multum perīcŭlum habent.
 7. Injusta bella aspĕra proelia habent.
 8. Multa oppĭda magna dona habent.
 9. Lātum regnum multa bella habet.
 10. Aurĕa scuta sacra templa ornant.

 1. An ancient temple adorns the large town.
 2. Much gold adorns the sacred shield.
 3. The small town loves the golden gift.
 4. The large kingdom has many rewards.
 5. The sacred temple has beautiful gifts.
 6. A great battle has many dangers.
 7. Many gifts adorn the ancient temple.
 8. The wide kingdoms have many towns.
 9. The ancient towns have sacred temples.
 10. The beautiful temples have much gold.

Adjectives of the Third Declension.

Exercise XIV.

Nouns and Adjectives declined like **Trabs**.

The Nouns and Verbs in this Exercise are the same as those in Exercises V. and XVII.

A.—1. Sapiens judex putat.
2. Ingens arx manet.
3. Audax custos currit.
4. Prudentes reges putant.
5. Ingentes trabes manent.
6. Praestantes milites cantant.

1. The immense beam remains.
2. The prudent king thinks.
3. The excellent soldier sings.
4. The bold guardians run.
5. The excellent citadels remain.
6. The wise judges think.

B.—1. Sapiens judex praestantem legem amat.
2. *Rex potens ingentem urbem amat.
3. Dux audax audāces milites amat.
4. Arx ingens inertem custōdem habet.
5. Prudentes duces praestantes milites habent.
6. Ingentes trabes audāces duces occīdunt.
7. Sapientes reges divītes obsīdes amant.
8. Audāces custōdes prudentem judĭcem cingunt.
9. Florentes urbes sapientem regem amant.
10. Rapāces milites inertes custōdes cingunt.

1. An immense beam kills the bold soldier.
2. The powerful general has rapacious soldiers.
3. The rapacious soldier kills the rich hostage.
4. The bold hostages kill the prudent general.
5. An excellent citadel adorns the immense cities.
6. Powerful kings have wise judges.
7. The excellent laws have powerful guardians.
8. Bold soldiers surround the powerful king.
9. Sluggish guardians surround the immense citadel.
10. The wise king loves flourishing cities.

* The ordinary position for an adjective is immediately *before* the substantive which it qualifies; but if the substantive is of one syllable, the adjective more frequently comes *after* the substantive.

Adjectives of the Third Declension.

Exercise XV.

Nouns and Adjectives declined like **Hostis**.

The Nouns and Verbs in this Exercise are the same as those in Exercises VI. and XVIII.

A.—1. Suavis vallis manet.
  2. Fidēlis canis currit.
  3. Memorabĭlis rupis manet.
  4. Tristes aves cantant.
  5. Nobĭles cives putant.
  6. Navāles turres manent.

  1. The sad bird sings.
  2. The naval tower remains.
  3. The noble citizen thinks.
  4. The memorable rocks remain.
  5. The faithful dogs run.
  6. The pleasant valleys remain.

B.—1. Fortis civis turpem hostem occīdit.
  2. Suavis vallis memorabĭlem rupem cingit.
  3. Fidēlis canis nobĭlem civem amat.
  4. Gravis fames debĭlem avem occīdit.
  5. Omnes hostes omnem classem cingunt.
  6. Memorabĭles rupes navālem turrem cingunt.
  7. Nobĭlis civis tristes aves amat.
  8. Omnes canes molles aures habent.
  9. Fortes cives fortem hostem cingunt.
  10. Tristes aves suavem vallem amant.

  1. The whole fleet surrounds the noble rock.
  2. The base dog kills the feeble birds.
  3. The sad bird has severe hunger.
  4. The brave enemy has a weak fleet.
  5. The memorable rock has naval towers.
  6. The sorrowful citizens kill the weak dog.
  7. All birds love the pleasant valleys.
  8. The faithful dogs love the brave citizens.
  9. Pleasant valleys surround the memorable rocks.
  10. The memorable valley has sad birds.

Neuter Adjectives of the Third Declension, with Neuter Nouns of the Third Declension.

Exercise XVI.

Neuter Nouns and Adjectives declined like
Opus and Mare.

The Nouns and Verbs in this Exercise are the same as those in Exercises VII. and XIX.

A.—1. Elĕgans dĕcus cadit.
   2. Ingens corpus manet.
   3. Ferox anĭmal currit.
   4. Suavia litŏra manent.
   5. Lĕvia retia cadunt.
   6. Difficilia nomĭna manent.

1. The pleasant shore remains.
2. The light net falls.
3. The difficult name remains.
4. The fierce animals run.
5. The elegant ornaments fall.
6. The immense bodies remain.

B.—1. Lĕve rete omne caput cingit.
   2. Crudēle mare suave litus habet.
   3. Ingens corpus lĕve caput habet.
   4. Elĕgans decus difficĭle nomen habet.
   5. Ferox anĭmal gracilia crura habet.
   6. Ingentia sidĕra difficilia nomĭna habent.
   7. Vilia decŏra humilia litŏra cingunt.
   8. Ferocia animalia suavia carmĭna amant.
   9. Humilia litŏra crudēle mare cingunt.
   10. Ingentia retia gracĭle gramen occĭdunt.

1. Cruel animals surround the pleasant shore.
2. An immense net surrounds the fierce animal.
3. The pleasant shore surrounds the cruel sea.
4. The fierce animal has a difficult name.
5. Slender grass surrounds the low shore.
6. Cheap ornaments surround the immense head.
7. Fierce animals have immense heads.
8. Light nets surround the cheap ornaments.
9. Immense heads have weak bodies.
10. Elegant animals have graceful legs.

Adjectives of the First and Second Declensions, with Nouns of the Third Declension.

Exercise XVII.

Adjectives declined like **Mensa, Dominus, Magister,** and **Puer,** with Nouns declined like **Trabs.**

The Nouns and Verbs in this Exercise are the same as those in Exercises V. and XIV.

A.—1. Doctus judex putat.
  2. Firma arx manet.
  3. Timĭdus custos currit.
  4. Boni reges putant.
  5. Magnae trabes manent.
  6. Nigri milĭtes cantant.

  1. The large beam remains.
  2. The good king thinks.
  3. The black soldier sings.
  4. The timid guardians run.
  5. The large citadels remain.
  6. The learned judges think.

B.—1. Justus judex bonam legem amat.
  2. Rex bonus magnam urbem amat.
  3. Dux perītus perītos milĭtes amat.
  4. Arx firma timĭdum custōdem habet.
  5. Benigni duces bonos milĭtes habent.
  6. Magnae trabes valĭdos duces occīdunt.
  7. Bellicōsi reges sacros obsĭdes amant.
  8. Libĕri custōdes doctum judĭcem cingunt.
  9. Pulchrae urbes bonum regem amant.
  10. Nigri milĭtes albos custōdes cingunt.

  1. A great beam kills the strong soldier.
  2. The good general has many soldiers.
  3. The strong soldier kills the timid hostage.
  4. The black hostages kill the skilful general.
  5. A white citadel adorns the sacred cities.
  6. Good kings have learned judges.
  7. The sacred laws have severe guardians.
  8. Skilful soldiers surround the kind king.
  9. Strong guardians surround the sacred citadel.
  10. The warlike king loves the beautiful cities.

Adjectives of the First and Second Declensions, with Nouns of the Third Declension.

Exercise XVIII.

Adjectives declined like **Mensa, Dominus, Magister,** and **Puer,** with Nouns declined like **Hostis.**

The Nouns and Verbs in this Exercise are the same as those in Exercises VI. and XV.

A.—1. Pulchra vallis manet.
2. Timĭdus canis currit.
3. Angusta rupes manet.
4. Laetae aves cantant.
5. Libĕri cives putant.
6. Altae turres manent.

1. The free bird sings.
2. The beautiful tower remains.
3. The joyful citizen thinks.
4. The memorable rocks remain.
5. The faithful dogs run.
6. The narrow valleys remain.

B.—1. Firmus civis molestum hostem occīdit.
2. Angusta vallis pulchram rupem cingit.
3. Caecus canis benignum civem amat.
4. Molesta fames raram avem occīdit.
5. Perniciōsi hostes claram classem cingunt.
6. Angustae rupes altam turrem cingunt.
7. Liber civis timĭdas aves amat.
8. Multi canes longas aures habent.
9. Bellicōsi cives perniciōsum hostem cingunt.
10. Laetae aves pulchram vallem amant.

1. The renowned fleet surrounds the high rock.
2. The troublesome dog kills the joyful birds.
3. The timid bird has destructive hunger.
4. The renowned enemy has a troublesome fleet.
5. The high rock has many towers.
6. The kind citizens kill the blind dog.
7. Timid birds love the beautiful valleys.
8. The blind dogs love the kind citizens.
9. Narrow valleys surround the high rocks.
10. The beautiful valley has rare birds.

Neuter Adjectives of the Second Declension, with Neuter Nouns of the Third Declension.

EXERCISE XIX.

Adjectives declined like **Regnum**, with Nouns declined like **Opus** and **Mare**.

The Nouns and Verbs in this Exercise are the same as those in Exercises VII. and XVI.

A.—1. Novum decus cadit.
    2. Valĭdum corpus manet.
    3. Timĭdum anĭmal currit.
    4. Angusta litŏra manent.
    5. Nova retia cadunt.
    6. Longa nomĭna manent.

1. The narrow shore remains.
2. The long net falls.
3. The new name remains.
4. The timid animals run.
5. The new ornaments fall.
6. The strong bodies remain.

B.—1. Novum rete parvum caput cingit.
    2. Latum mare longum litus habet.
    3. Valĭdum corpus doctum caput habet.
    4. Rarum decus novum nomen habet.
    5. Timĭdum anĭmal longa crura habet.
    6. Splendĭda sidĕra varia nomĭna habent.
    7. Innumĕra decŏra angusta litŏra cingunt.
    8. Multa anĭmalia jucunda carmĭna amant.
    9. Longa litŏra angustum mare cingunt.
  10. Pauca retia tenĕrum gramen occĭdunt.

1. Innumerable animals surround the narrow shore.
2. A wide net surrounds the timid animal.
3. The narrow shore surrounds the wide sea.
4. The rare animal has a long name.
5. Long grass surrounds the narrow shore.
6. Rare ornaments surround the splendid head.
7. Timid animals have long heads.
8. New nets surround the rare ornaments.
9. Learned heads have strong bodies.
10. The rare animals have many legs.

74 Adjectives of the First and Second Declensions
with Nouns of the Fourth Declension.

EXERCISE XX.

See Rule (d), page 54.

Adjectives declined like **Mensa, Dominus, Magister,** and **Regnum**, with Nouns declined like **Gradus** and **Genu.**

The Nouns and Verbs in this Exercise are the same as those in Exercises VIII. and XXVI.

A.—1. Longus lacus manet.
2. Nigra ficus cadit.
3. Tutus portus manet.
4. Pulchrae quercūs cadunt.
5. Magni exercĭtūs vĕniunt.
6. Docti magistrātūs putant.

1. The large army comes.
2. The beautiful oak falls.
3. The learned magistrate thinks.
4. The safe harbours remain.
5. The black figs fall.
6. The long lakes remain.

B.—1. Magnus exercĭtus valĭdum equitātum habet.
2. Rapĭdus cursus doctum magistrātum occīdit.
3. Valĭdus equitātus rapĭdum cursum amat.
4. Longus lacus tutos portūs habet.
5. Parva manus longam acum tenet.
6. Doctus magistrātus magnum currum habet.
7. Altae quercūs pulchros lacūs ornant.
8. Perītus peditātus longos arcūs habet.
9. Rarae ficūs acūta cornua cingunt.
10. Longae manūs altas quercūs tenent.

1. The skilful cavalry surrounds the strong infantry.
2. The skilful magistrate has a safe chariot.
3. The large army surrounds the skilful cavalry.
4. Safe harbours surround the long lake.
5. The beautiful horn holds the small figs.
6. Strong hands hold the sharp needles.
7. Beautiful oaks surround the safe harbour.
8. The learned magistrates have large chariots.
9. Large armies have strong cavalry.
10. Long bows adorn strong hands.

Adjectives of the First and Second Declensions, with Nouns of the Fifth Declension.

Exercise XXI.

Adjectives declined like **Mensa, Dominus,** and **Magister,** with Nouns declined like **Dies.**

The Nouns and Verbs in this Exercise are the same as those in Exercises IX. and XXVII.

A.—1. Serēna facies manet.
2. Laeta dies vĕnit.
3. Pulchra res manet.
4. Jucundae effigies manent.
5. Multae spes manent.
6. Longae acies manent.

1. The beautiful likeness remains.
2. Joyful hope comes.
3. The long line-of-battle remains.
4. Many things remain.
5. The long days come.
6. The calm faces remain.

B.—1. Serēna fides laetam spem habet.
2. Serēnus dies jucundum merīdiem habet.
3. Mala segnities longum diem occīdit.
4. Pulchra facies jucundam effigiem habet.
5. Longa acies angustam planitiem cingit.
6. Rapĭda pernicies res multas cingit.
7. Laeta spes multos dies cingit.
8. Serēna facies magnam spem habet.
9. Pulchra dies lātam planitiem ornat.
10. Imprŏba segnities multam spem occīdit.

1. Much hope surrounds the fine day.
2. The long day has calm hope.
3. The narrow plain has a long line-of-battle.
4. Many things love fine days.
5. Many days have a pleasant noon.
6. A long hope adorns many things.
7. A wide plain surrounds the narrow line-of-battle.
8. A pleasant noon adorns many days.
9. Calm faces have a joyful hope.
10. Joyful hope kills much slothfulness.

Adjectives of the Third Declension, with Nouns of the First Declension.

Exercise XXII.

Adjectives declined like **Trabs** or **Hostis**, with Nouns declined like **Mensa**.

The Nouns and Verbs in this Exercise are the same as those in Exercises I. and X.

A.—1. Gracĭlis filia currit.
 2. Gracīles filiae currunt.
 3. Hilăres femĭnae cantant.
 4. Hilăris femĭna cantat.
 5. Sapientes puellae currunt.
 6. Sapiens puella cantat.

 1. The wise woman runs.
 2. The wise women run.
 3. The cheerful girls sing.
 4. The slender daughter sings.
 5. The cheerful girl runs.
 6. The slender daughters sing.

B.—1. Dives regīna ingentem corōnam habet.
 2. Gracĭlis puella suavem rosam habet.
 3. Hilăris femĭna gracĭlem filiam habet.
 4. Fidēlis colonia debīles columbas habet.
 5. Mites columbae elegantes alas habent.
 6. Felīces insŭlae ingentes colonias habent.
 7. Hilăres puellae suaves rosas habent.
 8. Dīves colonia felīces insŭlas habet.
 9. Sapiens regīna gracīles filias habet.
 10. Felix insŭla ingentes columbas habet.

 1. The cheerful girl has a gentle dove.
 2. The immense colony has wise women.
 3. The gentle dove has feeble wings.
 4. The fruitful island has faithful colonies.
 5. The slender girls have gentle doves.
 6. The cheerful women have sweet roses.
 7. The faithful colonies have immense islands.
 8. The rich queens have elegant crowns.
 9. The fruitful islands have slender doves.
 10. The slender women have cheerful daughters.

Adjectives of the Third Declension, with Nouns of the Second Declension.

Exercise XXIII.

Adjectives declined like **Trabs** and **Hostis**, with Nouns declined like **Dominus**.

The Nouns and Verbs in this Exercise are the same as those in Exercises II. and XI.

A.—1. Diligens servus currit.
    2. Diligentes servi currunt.
    3. Utiles amici cantant.
    4. Utilis amicus currit.
    5. Dives avus cantat.
    6. Divites avi currunt.

    1. The rich friend sings.
    2. The rich friends run.
    3. The useful slaves sing.
    4. The diligent grandfathers sing.
    5. The useful slave sings.
    6. The diligent grandfather runs.

B.—1. Prudens amicus felicem hortum amat.
    2. Potens dominus utiles servos habet.
    3. Fideles servi veloces equos amant.
    4. Crudelis inimicus ingentem gladium habet.
    5. Dives avus suaves hortos habet.
    6. Divites domini diligentes filios habent.
    7. Veloces equi veloces fluvios amant.
    8. Sapientes avi prudentes amicos amant.
    9. Fidelis servus velocem equum amat.
  10. Felix hortus ingentem fluvium habet.

    1. The wise grandfather has a useful horse.
    2. The faithful friend loves the prudent son.
    3. The diligent son has a wise grandfather.
    4. The rich lord has useful sons.
    5. The cruel enemies have immense swords.
    6. The rich friends have fruitful gardens.
    7. The pleasant gardens have immense rivers.
    8. The prudent slaves love the powerful lord.
    9. The diligent sons have wise grandfathers.
  10. The faithful friends have cruel enemies.

Adjectives of the Third Declension, with Nouns of the Second Declension.

Exercise XXIV.

Adjectives declined like **Trabs** and **Hostis**, with Nouns declined like **Magister** and **Puer**.

The Nouns and Verbs in this Exercise are the same as those in Exercises III. and XII.

A.—1. Diligens puer currit.
  2. Diligentes pueri currunt.
  3. Fidelis minister cantat.
  4. Felix gener currit.
  5. Sapientes soceri cantant.
  6. Utiles ministri currunt.

  1. The useful servant runs.
  2. The useful servants sing.
  3. The happy boy sings.
  4. The wise father-in-law runs.
  5. The happy boys sing.
  6. The wise sons-in-law run.

B.—1. Praestans magister fidelem ministrum habet.
  2. Hilaris socer diligentem puerum amat.
  3. Sapiens puer utilem librum habet.
  4. Prudens gener mendacem ministrum habet.
  5. Diligens socer felicem agrum habet.
  6. Sapiens magister utiles libros habet.
  7. Divites soceri diligentes generos amant.
  8. Praestantes magistri fideles ministros habent.
  9. Hilares pueri suaves agros amant.
  10. Fidelis magister diligentes pueros habet.

  1. The faithful servant has a wise father-in-law.
  2. The rich son-in-law has cheerful boys.
  3. The prudent master has an excellent book.
  4. The cheerful boy loves the fruitful fields.
  5. The rich father-in-law has a diligent son-in-law.
  6. The wise sons-in-law have prudent fathers-in-law.
  7. The diligent boys have excellent books.
  8. The faithful sons-in-law have false servants.
  9. The wise boys love the pleasant field.
  10. The diligent fathers-in-law have fruitful fields.

Neuter Adjectives of the Third Declension, with Neuter Nouns of the Second Declension.

Exercise XXV.

Adjectives declined like **Opus** and **Mare**, with Nouns declined like **Regnum**.

The Nouns and Verbs in this Exercise are the same as those in Exercises IV. and XIII.

A.—1. Potens regnum manet.
2. Elegantia oppida manent.
3. Ingentia templa florent.
4. Elegans oppidum manet.
5. Potentia regna manent.
6. Elegans templum floret.

1. The powerful town flourishes.
2. The elegant temple remains.
3. The immense kingdoms flourish.
4. The elegant temples remain.
5. The immense kingdom flourishes.
6. The powerful towns flourish.

B.—1. Ingens oppidum elegans templum habet.
2. Elegans templum grave aurum habet.
3. Bellum civile atrocia praemia habet.
4. Tenue aurum praestans templum ornat.
5. Elegantia templa levia scuta habent.
6. Gravia proelia atrox periculum habent.
7. Ferocia bella atrocia proelia habent.
8. Florentia oppida utilia dona habent.
9. Potens regnum ferocia bella habet.
10. Ingentia scuta elegantia templa ornant.

1. An elegant temple adorns the immense town.
2. Heavy gold adorns the light shield.
3. The flourishing town loves the useful gift.
4. The immense kingdom has useful rewards.
5. The excellent temple has immense gifts.
6. A fierce battle has stern dangers.
7. Useful gifts adorn the elegant temple.
8. The flourishing kingdoms have immense towns.
9. The powerful towns have excellent temples.
10. The immense temples have thin gold.

80 Adjectives of the Third Declension, with Nouns of the Fourth Declension.

Exercise XXVI.

See Rule (d), page 54.

Adjectives declined like **Trabs** and **Hostis**, with Nouns declined like **Gradus** and **Genu**.

The Nouns and Verbs in this Exercise are the same as those in Exercises VIII. and XX.

A.—1. Iners lacus manet.
   2. Dulcis ficus cadit.
   3. Utilis portus manet.
   4. Ingentes quercūs cadunt.
   5. Audāces exercĭtūs vĕniunt.
   6. Fidĕles magistrātūs putant.

   1. The bold army comes.
   2. The immense oak falls.
   3. The faithful magistrate thinks.
   4. The useful harbours remain.
   5. The sweet figs fall.
   6. The sluggish lakes remain.

B.—1. Ingens exercĭtus fortem equitātum habet.
   2. Velox cursus debĭlem magistrātum occīdit.
   3. Audax equitātus velōcem cursum amat.
   4. Ingens lacus praestantes portūs habet.
   5. Tenuis manus utĭlem acum tenet.
   6. Fidĕlis magistrātus velōcem currum habet.
   7. Ingentes quercūs inertes lacūs ornant.
   8. Audax peditātus lĕves arcūs habet.
   9. Dulces ficūs ingentia cornua cingunt.
   10. Tenues manūs tenues quercūs tenent.

   1. The swift cavalry surrounds the brave infantry.
   2. The feeble magistrate has a light chariot.
   3. The bold army surrounds the sluggish cavalry.
   4. Excellent harbours surround the immense lake.
   5. The slender horn holds the sweet figs.
   6. Swift hands hold the useful needles.
   7. Slender oaks surround the excellent harbour.
   8. The faithful magistrates have swift chariots.
   9. The immense armies have bold cavalry.
   10. Light bows adorn slender hands.

Adjectives of the Third Declension, with Nouns of the Fifth Declension.

Exercise XXVII.

Adjectives declined like **Trabs** and **Hostis**, with Nouns declined like **Dies**.

The Nouns and Verbs in this Exercise are the same as those in Exercises IX. and XXI.

A.—1. Tenuis facies manet.
2. Brevis dies vĕnit.
3. Praestans res manet.
4. Praestantes effigies manent.
5. Hilăres spes manent.
6. Ingentes acies manent.

1. The excellent likeness remains.
2. Cheerful hope comes.
3. The immense line-of-battle remains.
4. Excellent things remain.
5. The short days come.
6. The slender faces remain.

B.—1. Hilăris fides fortem spem habet.
2. Brevis dies debĭlem merĭdĭem habet.
3. Turpis segnities velōcem diem occīdit.
4. Tenuis facies praestantem effigiem habet.
5. Ingens acies felīcem planitiem cingit.
6. Simĭlis pernicies res simĭles cingit.
7. Hilăris spes brĕves dies cingit.
8. Talis facies tenuem spem habet.
9. Hilăris dies ingentem planitiem ornat.
10. Iners segnities hilărem spem occīdit.

1. Strong hope surrounds the happy day.
2. The swift day has immense hope.
3. The fruitful plain has an immense line-of-battle.
4. Happy things love cheerful days.
5. Short days have a feeble noon.
6. A cheerful hope adorns excellent things.
7. An immense plain surrounds the short line-of-battle.
8. A feeble noon adorns short days.
9. Such faces have a feeble hope.
10. Cheerful hope kills sluggish slothfulness.

Exercise XXVIII.

I. *The Cardinal Numerals.*

A.—1. Corpus căput unum habet.
2. Domĭnus centum servos habet.
3. Mille milĭtes urbem cingunt.
4. Una insŭla novem fluvios habet.
5. Duo discipŭli duodĕcim libros habent.
6. Tres muri tredĕcim turres habent.
7. Viginti rupes duas naves cingunt.
8. Tria templa tres portas habent.

1. The head has one body.
2. Seven slaves surround the lord.
3. Three gates adorn the three temples.
4. Twenty scholars have one hundred books.
5. The two walls have twenty towers.
6. Thirteen rocks surround the nine ships.
7. The two islands have twelve rivers.
8. The masters have twenty slaves.

II. *The Ordinal Numerals.*

B.—1. Socer secundum genĕrum habet.
2. Milĭtes duodecĭmam turrem cingunt.
3. Puĕri quintum quercum cingunt.
4. Prima puella primum praemium habet.
5. Nŏnus murus septĭmum murum cingit.
6. Decĭmus discipŭlus vicesĭmum librum habet.
7. Sexta insŭla quartum portum habet.
8. Centesĭmum scutum tertium templum ornat.

1. The soldiers surround the fifth tower.
2. The girls surround the tenth oak.
3. The hundredth scholar has the twentieth book.
4. The twelfth shield adorns the seventh temple.
5. The third boy has the fourth reward.
6. The son-in-law has (his) first father-in-law.
7. The ninth island has the sixth harbour.
8. The second wall surrounds the first wall.

The Verb Sum.

Exercise XXIX.

The Indicative of the Verb Sum.

Rule 4.—When two Nouns in Latin are connected by the verb "To be," they are put in the same case: as, Brĭtannĭă est insŭlă, *Britain is an island.* Use the Nominative case after the verb "To be."

A.—1. Columba est avis.
    2. Puer est discipŭlus.
    3. Amīcus ĕrat domĭnus.
    4. Elephanti sunt animalia.
    5. Puer ĕrit nauta.
    6. Judĭces ĕrant duces.
    7. Cives ĕrunt obsĭdes.
    8. Segnities ĕrit pernicies.

1. The general is a citizen.
2. Doves are birds.
3. The boys will be sailors.
4. The hostages were citizens.
5. The general will be the judge.
6. Indolence is (his) ruin.
7. The lords were friends.
8. The elephant is an animal.

B.—1. Māter fuit puella.
    2. Dux fuĕrat obses.
    3. Milītes fuĕrint cives.
    4. Păter fuĕrit nauta.
    5. Domĭni fuĕrant amĭci.
    6. Puĕri fuĕrunt nautae.
    7. Segnities fuĕrit pernicies.
    8. Gener fuĕrat socer.

1. Indolence has been (his) ruin.
2. The mother had been a girl.
3. The soldiers had been hostages.
4. The father has been a sailor.
5. The lord had been a hostage.
6. The fathers-in-law have been sons-in-law.
7. The citizens had been friends.
8. The boys have been sailors.

First Conjugation.—Active Voice.

EXERCISE XXX.
THE PRESENT, IMPERFECT, AND FUTURE-SIMPLE TENSES, INDICATIVE.

The Nouns and Verbs in this (A.) *Exercise are the same as those in Exercise XXXI.* (A.).

A.—1. Femĭna saltat.
2. Dux pugnābit.
3. Custos vigilābat.
4. Elephanti ambulābunt.
5. Aves volant.
6. Reges regnābant.

1. The king reigns.
2. The elephant was walking.
3. The bird will fly.
4. The generals will fight.
5. The women were dancing.
6. The guardians watch.

B.—1. Quercus vallem ornat.
2. Regīna ducem laudābit.
3. Domĭnus servos vituperābat.
4. Decŏra caput ornant.
5. Femĭna filiam vituperābit.
6. Duces urbes firmābant.
7. Reges arces aedificābunt.
8. Animalia gramen amant.
9. Milĭtes urbem intrābant.
10. Hostes arcem firmābunt.

1. The queen was praising the soldiers.
2. The king will build the cities.
3. The animal loves grass.
4. The general will strengthen the citadel.
5. The oaks adorn the valleys.
6. The general will strengthen the city.
7. The daughters were praising the women.
8. The lords find-fault-with the slaves.
9. The ornaments will adorn the queen.
10. The soldiers were entering the citadel.

Exercise XXXI.

The Perfect, Pluperfect, and Future-Perfect Tenses, Indicative.

The Nouns and Verbs in this (A.) *Exercise are the same as those in Exercise XXX.* (A.).

A.—1. Femĭna saltāvit.
2. Dux pugnavĕrit.
3. Custos vigĭlavĕrat.
4. Elephanti ambulavĕrant.
5. Aves volavĕrint.
6. Reges regnavĕrunt.

1. The king will have reigned.
2. The elephant had walked.
3. The bird has flown.
4. The generals have fought.
5. The women will have danced.
6. The guardians had watched.

B.—1. Exercĭtus urbes expugnavĕrat.
2. Puer laudem parāvit.
3. Dux arcem firmavĕrat.
4. Equus agrum intrāvit.
5. Avis vallem intravĕrat.
6. Hostes classem paravĕrunt.
7. Reges urbes aedificavĕrint.
8. Canes hortos intravĕrant.
9. Cives exercĭtum laudavĕrint.
10. Milĭtes arces oppugnavĕrunt.

1. The soldier will have praised the army.
2. The dog entered the garden.
3. The army had attacked the enemy.
4. The king will have built the cities.
5. The citizen praised the army.
6. The horses had entered the fields.
7. The generals have strengthened the citadels.
8. The boys had gained praise.
9. The enemy attacked the citadels.
10. The birds will have entered the valleys.

Second Conjugation.—Active Voice.

Exercise XXXII.

The Present, Imperfect, and Future-Simple Tenses, Indicative.

The Nouns and Verbs in this (A.) *Exercise are the same as those in Exercise XXXIII.* (A.).

A.—1. Puer valet.
2. Quercus manēbit.
3. Puella tacēbat.
4. Rosae florēbunt.
5. Judĭces sĕdēbant.
6. Gladii fulgent.

1. The judge will sit.
2. The sword glitters.
3. The rose was blooming.
4. The oaks remain.
5. The boys will-be-silent.
6. The girls were-in-good-health.

B.—1. Magister puĕrum monēbat.
2. Canis avem terrēbit.
3. Exercĭtus arcem delēbat.
4. Servus canem coercet.
5. Tempus quercum delēbit.
6. Bellum exercĭtum delet.
7. Puĕri columbas terrēbant.
8. Animalia cornua habēbunt.
9. Manūs arcūs tenēbant.
10. Femĭnae puellas docent.

1. The dog frightens the dove.
2. The hand will hold the bow.
3. The animal has horns.
4. The woman was teaching the girl.
5. The oak will frighten the animal.
6. The slaves restrain the dogs.
7. Wars will destroy the armies.
8. The boys have birds.
9. The masters will teach the boys.
10. The dogs were frightening the birds.

Exercise XXXIII.

The Perfect, Pluperfect and Future-Perfect Tenses, Indicative.

The Nouns and Verbs in this (A.) Exercise are the same as those in Exercise XXXII. (A.).

A.—1. Puer valuĕrat.
    2. Quercus mansĕrit.
    3. Puella tacuit.
    4. Rosae floruĕrant.
    5. Judices sedĕrint.
    6. Gladii fulsĕrunt.

1. The judge will have sat.
2. The sword has glittered.
3. The rose had bloomed.
4. The oaks have remained.
5. The boys will-have-been-silent.
6. The girls had-been-in-good-health.

B.—1. Manus quercum movĕrat.
    2. Custos obsidem coercuit.
    3. Fames servum delevĕrit.
    4. Hortus rosas habuit.
    5. Mare equos terruĕrat.
    6. Magistri pueros docuĕrunt.
    7. Magistratūs ministros monuĕrint.
    8. Puella dona tenuĕrat.
    9. Hostes arcem delevĕrint.
    10. Manus columbam tenuĕrunt.

1. The magistrate warned the boy.
2. The enemy had destroyed the citadel.
3. The sea frightened the horse.
4. The master had a garden.
5. Hunger will have destroyed the doves.
6. The hands moved the oak.
7. The guardians had restrained the hostages.
8. The girls will have held the roses.
9. The master had warned the boys.
10. The slaves have destroyed the citadel.

Third Conjugation.—Active Voice.

Exercise XXXIV.

The Present, Imperfect, and Future-Simple Tenses, Indicative.

The Nouns and Verbs in this (A.) *Exercise are the same as those in Exercise XXXV.* (A.).

A.—1. Rex regit.
    2. Fluvius fluet.
    3. Puer ludēbat.
    4. Equi ĕdent.
    5. Manūs scribunt.
    6. Puellae pingēbant.

1. The hand will paint.
2. The horse eats.
3. The girl was writing.
4. The rivers were flowing.
5. Kings rule.
6. Boys will play.

B.—1. Rex urbes regit.
    2. Dux exercĭtum ducēbat.
    3. Servus agrum colet.
    4. Rete caput cingēbat.
    5. Fluvius mare petit.
    6. Aurum scuta teget.
    7. Hostes aciem instruēbant.
    8. Domĭni equos ement.
    9. Puer segnitiem vincet.
   10. Manūs quercūs cingunt.

1. Gold covers the shield.
2. The general was arranging the line-of-battle.
3. The lord will buy the horse.
4. The oaks will cover the field.
5. The net surrounds the hands.
6. The shields were covering the heads.
7. The generals will lead the armies.
8. The slaves were cultivating the field.
9. The boys will conquer indolence.
10. The rivers seek the sea.

Third Conjugation.—Active Voice.

Exercise XXXV.

The Perfect, Pluperfect, and Future-Perfect Tenses, Indicative.

The Nouns and Verbs in this (A.) Exercise are the same as those in Exercise XXXIV. (A.).

A.—1. Rex rexĕrat.
2. Fluvius fluxit.
3. Puer luserit.
4. Equi ĕdĕrant.
5. Manūs scripsĕrint.
6. Puellae pinxĕrunt.

1. The hand had painted.
2. The horse will have eaten.
3. The girl has written.
4. The rivers had flowed.
5. The kings have ruled.
6. The boys will have played.

B.—1. Dux exercĭtum duxit.
2. Equus gramen ĕdĕrit.
3. Puer segnitiem vīcit.
4. Scutum milĭtem defendĕrat.
5. Equi currūs traxĕrunt.
6. Puĕri praemia petīvĕrant.
7. Milĭtes templum cinxĕrunt.
8. Reges leges scripsĕrint.
9. Filii equos ēmĕrant.
10. Rupes classem cinxĕrunt.

1. The boy will have conquered indolence.
2. The soldier led the horse.
3. The son had bought the shield.
4. The fleet will have surrounded the rocks.
5. The boy sought the reward.
6. The fleet had defended the army.
7. The horses have eaten the grass.
8. Shields had surrounded the temples.
9. The king has written the law.
10. The soldiers defended the generals.

Fourth Conjugation.—Active Voice.

Exercise XXXVI.

The Present, Imperfect, and Future-Simple Tenses, Indicative.

The Nouns and Verbs in this (A.) Exercise are the same as those in Exercise XXXVII. (A.).

A.—1. Avus dormiēbat.
2. Bellum evĕniet.
3. Avis audit.
4. Amīci vĕniēbant.
5. Custōdes dormient.
6. Dies vĕniunt.

1. The guardian sleeps.
2. The day will come.
3. The friend was coming.
4. Wars will happen.
5. The grandfathers hear.
6. The birds were sleeping.

B.—1. Avus puĕrum puniet.
2. Puer avum repĕrit.
3. Civis canem erudiēbat.
4. Canis aves reperiet.
5. Gramen equum nutrit.
6. Custōdes coloniam custodiunt.
7. Milītes arces munient.
8. Equĭtes vallem custodiēbant.
9. Duces pedĭtes erudiunt.
10. Servi domĭnum sepeliēbant.

1. The grass was nourishing the bird.
2. The soldier will guard the citizen.
3. The horse finds the grass.
4. The master will train the boys.
5. The dog was guarding the grandfather.
6. Birds will find the valleys.
7. The horse-soldiers were training the horses.
8. The foot-soldiers fortify the citadel.
9. The boys were burying the bird.
10. The soldiers will guard the colonies.

Fourth Conjugation.—Active Voice.

Exercise XXXVII.

The Perfect, Pluperfect, and Future-Perfect Tenses, Indicative.

The Nouns and Verbs in this (A.) *Exercise are the same as those in Exercise XXXVI.* (A.).

A.—1. Avus dormīvĕrat.
    2. Bellum evēnit (*perf.*).
    3. Avis audīvĕrit.
    4. Amīci vēnĕrint.
    5. Custōdes dormīvĕrant.
    6. Dies vēnĕrunt.

1. The guardian will have slept.
2. The day has come.
3. The friend had come.
4. Wars have happened.
5. The grandfathers had heard.
6. The birds will have slept.

B.—1. Femĭna filias erudīvit.
    2. Judex legem scivĕrit.
    3. Servus puĕros erudīvĕrat.
    4. Socer civem vestīvit.
    5. Puer librum finīvĕrit.
    6. Dux arcem munīvit.
    7. Domĭni servos vinxĕrant.
    8. Gramen insŭlas vestīvit.
    9. Amīci puellas vestīvĕrant.
  10. Servi domĭnum sepelivĕrunt.

1. The judge bound the citizen.
2. The lord had trained the slaves.
3. The son-in-law clothed (his) enemy.
4. The citizens have buried the judge.
5. The generals will have fortified the island.
6. The friends had buried the citizen.
7. Grass has clothed the island.
8. The judges knew the law.
9. The daughters will have trained the girl.
10. The boys have finished the book.

PART IV.
VOCABULARIES.

m. = masculine.
f. = feminine.
n. = neuter.
c. = common gender, that is, masculine and feminine.

As the A. vocabularies should be learnt before the B. vocabularies, some words are necessarily repeated.

Vocabulary 1.
A.
fēmĭna, ae, f. 1. a woman.
fīlĭa, ae, f. 1. a daughter.
pŭella, ae, f. 1. a girl.

B.
āla, ae, f. 1. a wing.
cŏlōnĭa, ae, f. 1. a colony.
cŏlumba, ae, f. 1. a dove.
cŏrōna, ae, f. 1. a crown.
insŭla, ae, f. 1. an island.
rēgīna, ae, f. 1. a queen.
rŏsa, ae, f. 1. a rose.

Vocabulary 2.
A.
ămīcus, i, m. 2. a friend.
ăvus, i, m. 2. a grandfather.
servus, i, m. 2. a slave.

B.
dŏmĭnus, i, m. 2. a lord, master.
ĕquus, i, m. 2. a horse.
fīlĭus, i, m. 2. a son.
flŭvĭus, ii, m. 2. a river.
glădĭus, ii, m. 2. a sword.
hortus, i, m. 2. a garden.
ĭnĭmīcus, i, m. 2. an enemy.

Vocabulary 3.
A.
(1.) Declined like *Măgistĕr*.
mĭnister, tri, m. 2. a servant.

(2.) Declined like *Pŭĕr*.
gĕner, ĕri, m. 2. a son-in-law.
pŭer, ĕri, m. 2. a boy.
sŏcer, ĕri, m. 2. a father-in-law.

B.
(1.) Declined like *Măgistĕr*.
ăger, ăgri, m. 2. a field.
lĭber, libri, m. 2. a book.
măgister, tri, m. 2. a master, teacher.

Vocabulary 4.
A.
oppĭdum, i, n. 2. a town.
regnum, i, n. 2. a kingdom.
templum, i, n. 2. a temple.

B.
aurum, i, n. 2. gold.
bellum, i, n. 2. war.
dōnum, i, n. 2. a gift.
pĕrīcŭlum, i, n. 2. danger.
praemĭum, ii, n. 2. a reward.
proelĭum, ii, n. 2. battle.
scūtum, i, n. 2. a shield.

Vocabulary 5.

A.

arx, arcis, *f.* 3.   *a citadel.*
custos, custōdis, *a guardian.*
  c. 3.
jūdex, jūdĭcis, *c.* 3. *a judge.*
mīlĕs, mīlĭtis, *c.* 3. *a soldier.*
rex, rēgis, *m.* 3.   *a king.*
trabs, trăbis, *f.* 3. *a beam.*

B.

dux, dŭcis, *c.* 3.   *a leader,*
                general.
lex, lēgis, *f.* 3.   *a law.*
obsĕs, obsĭdis, *c.* 3. *a hostage.*
urbs, urbis, *f.* 3. *a city.*

Vocabulary 6.

A.

ăvis, is, *f.* 3.   *a bird.*
cănis, is, *c.* 3.   *a dog.*
cīvis, is, *c.* 3.   *a citizen.*
rūpēs, is, *f.* 3.   *a rock.*
turris, is, *f.* 3.   *a tower.*
vallis, is, *f.* 3.   *a valley.*

B.

auris, is, *f.* 3.   *an ear.*
classis, is, *f.* 3.   *a fleet.*
fămēs, is, *f.* 3.   *hunger.*
hostis, is, *c.* 3.   *an enemy (pub-*
                lic enemy).

Vocabulary 7.

A.

(*a.*) Declined like *Ŏpŭs.*

corpus, ŏris, *n.* 3. *a body.*
dĕcus, ŏris, *n.* 3. *an ornament.*
lītus, ŏris, *n.* 3. *a shore.*
nōmen, ĭnis, *n.* 3. *a name.*
*ănĭmăl, ālis, *n.* 3. *an animal.*

---

* *In Neuter nouns in* ĕ, ăl, *and* ăr (*gen.* ăris), *the abl. sing. ends in* ī, *the gen. pl. in* ĭum; *the nom., acc., and voc. pl. in* ĭa.

(*b.*) Declined like *Mărĕ.*
*rēte, is, *n.* 3.   *a net.*

B.

(*a.*) Declined like *Ŏpŭs.*

căput, ĭtis, *n.* 3.   *a head.*
carmen, ĭnis, *n.* 3. *a song.*
crūs, crūris, *n.* 3. *a leg.*
grāmen, ĭnis, *n.* 3. *grass.*
sīdus, ĕris, *n.* 3. *a star.*

(*b.*) Declined like *Mărĕ.*
* mărĕ, is, *n.* 3.   *the sea.*

Vocabulary 8.

See Rule (*d*), page 54.

A.

exercĭtus, ūs, *m.* 4. *an army.*
fīcus, ūs, *f.* 4.   *a fig.*
lăcus, ūs, *m.* 4. *a lake.*
măgistrătus, ūs, *a magistrate.*
  m. 4.
portus, ūs, *m.* 4. *a harbour.*
quercus, ūs, *f.* 4. *an oak.*

B.

ăcus, ūs, *f.* 4.   *a needle.*
arcus, ūs, *m.* 4. *a bow.*
currus, ūs, *m.* 4. *a chariot.*
cursus, ūs, *m.* 4. *running.*
ĕquĭtātus, ūs, *m.* 4. *cavalry.*
mănus, ūs, *f.* 4. *a hand.*
pĕdĭtātus, ūs, *m.* 4. *infantry.*

cornu, ūs, *n.* 4. *a horn.*

Vocabulary 9.

See Rule (*c*), page 54.

A.

ăcĭēs, ēī, *f.* 5.   *a line-of-battle.*
dĭēs, ēī, *m.* and *f.* 5. *a day.*
effĭgĭēs, ēī, *f.* 5. *a likeness.*
făcĭēs, ēī, *f.* 5. *a face, counte-*
              nance.
rēs, ēī, *f.* 5.   *a thing.*
spēs, ēī, *f.* 5.   *hope.*

B.

fĭdēs, ēi, f. 5.   faith, fidelity.
mĕrīdĭēs, ēi, m. 5. mid-day, noon.
pernĭcĭēs, ēi, f. 5. destruction,
plānĭtĭēs, ēi, f. 5. a plain. [ruin.
segnĭtĭēs, ēi, f. 5. slothfulness, in-
                    dolence.

Vocabulary 10.

A.

bŏnus, a, um,   good.
tĭmĭdus, a, um,   timid.

pulcher, chra,   beautiful.
   chrum,

B.

albus, a, um,   white.
magnus, a, um,   great, large.
multus, a, um,   much, many.
parvus, a, um,   small, little.

līber, ĕra, ĕrum,   free.

Vocabulary 11.

A.

doctus, a, um,   learned.
vălĭdus, a, um,   strong (able to
                   perform).

B.

bĕnignus, a, um,   kind.
indoctus, a, um,   unlearned.
lātus, a, um,   wide, broad.
mălus, a, um,   bad, wicked.
pĕrītus, a, um,   skilful.

Vocabulary 12.

A.

(a.) Declined like Nĭgĕr.
aeger, gra, grum, sick.
nĭger, gra, grum, black.

(b.) Declined like Tĕnĕr.
asper, ĕra, ĕrum, rough, rugged.
līber, ĕra, ĕrum, free.

B.

(a.) Declined like Nĭgĕr.
noster, tra, trum,   our, ours.
săcer, cra, crum,   sacred.
vester, tra, trum,   your, yours.

(b.) Declined like Tĕnĕr.
tĕner, ĕra, ĕrum,   tender.

Vocabulary 13.

A.

antīquus, a, um,   ancient.
magnus, a, um,   great, large.
parvus, a, um,   small, little.

B.

aurĕus, a, um,   golden.
injustus, a, um,   unjust.

Vocabulary 14.

A.

audax, ācis,   bold.
ingens, entis,   immense.
praestans, antis,   excellent.
prūdens, entis,   prudent.
săpĭens, entis,   wise.

B.

dīvĕs, ĭtis,   rich.
flōrens, entis,   flourishing.
ĭners, ertis,   helpless, sluggish.
pŏtens, entis,   powerful.
răpax, ācis,   rapacious.

Vocabulary 15.

A.

fĭdēlis, e,   faithful.
mĕmŏrābĭlis, e,   to be remembered,
                  memorable.
nāvālis, e,   naval.
nōbĭlis, e,   distinguished.
suāvis, e,   sweet, delightful,
                  pleasant.
tristis, e,   sad, sorrowful.

B.

dēbĭlis, e,   feeble.
fortis, e,   strong, brave.

grăvis, e,   *heavy, severe.*
mollis, e,   *soft.*
omnis, e,   *all, every, whole.*
turpis, e,   *base, disgraceful.*

Vocabulary 16.

A.

(a.) Declined, in the neuter, like Ŏpŭs (*except that the abl. sing. ends in i and e*).

ēlĕgans, antis,   *elegant, exquisite.*
fĕrox, ōcis,   *fierce, spirited.*

(b.) Declined, in the neuter, like Mărĕ.

diffĭcĭlis, e,   *difficult.*
lĕvis, e,   *light (not heavy).*

B.

Declined, in the neuter, like Mărĕ.

crūdēlis, e,   *cruel.*
grăcĭlis, e,   *thin, slender.*
hŭmĭlis, e,   *low.*
vīlis, e,   *cheap, common.*

Vocabulary 17.

A.

firmus, a, um,   *strong (from position), immovable.*

B.

bellĭcōsus, a, um,   *warlike.*
justus, a, um,   *just.*
sĕvĕrus, a, um,   *severe.*

Vocabulary 18.

A.

altus, a, um,   *high, deep.*
angustus, a, um,   *narrow.*
laetus, a, um,   *joyful.*

B.

caecus, a, um,   *blind.*
clārus, a, um,   *clear, renowned.*
mŏlestus, a, um,   *troublesome.*
pernĭcĭōsus, a, um,   *destructive.*
rārus, a, um,   *rare.*

Vocabulary 19.

A.

longus, a, um,   *long.*
nŏvus, a, um,   *new.*

B.

innŭmĕrus, a, um,   *innumerable.*
jūcundus, a, um,   *pleasant.*
paucus, a, um,   *few.*
splendĭdus, a, um,   *splendid, bright.*
vărĭus, a, um,   *various.*

Vocabulary 20.

A.

tūtus, a, um,   *safe.*

B.

ăcūtus, a, um,   *sharp.*
răpĭdus, a, um,   *rapid.*

Vocabulary 21.

A.

jūcundus, a, um,   *pleasant.*
multus, a, um,   *much, many.*
sĕrēnus, a, um,   *clear, calm.*

B.

imprŏbus, a, um,   *wicked.*

Vocabulary 22.

A.

grăcĭlis, e,   *thin, slender.*
hĭlăris, e,   *cheerful.*

B.

fēlix, īcis,   happy, fortunate, fruitful.
mītis, e,   mild.

Vocabulary 23.
A.
dīlĭgens, entis,   diligent, careful.
dīvĕs, ĭtis,   rich.
ūtĭlis, e,   useful.

B.
vēlox, ōcis,   swift.

Vocabulary 24.
A.
fēlix, īcis,   happy, fortunate, fruitful.

B.
mendax, ācis,   lying, false.

Vocabulary 25.
A.
pŏtens, entis,   powerful.

B.
atrox, ōcis,   stern, sanguinary, cruel.
cīvīlis, e,   belonging to a citizen, civil.
tĕnŭis, e,   thin, delicate, slender.

Vocabulary 26.
A.
dulcis, e,   sweet, pleasant (to the taste).
ĭners, ĭnertis,   helpless, sluggish.

Vocabulary 27.
A.
brĕvis, e,   short.
tĕnŭis, e,   thin, delicate, slender.

B.
sĭmĭlis, e,   like.
tālis, e,   of that sort, such.
turpis, e,   base, disgraceful.

Vocabulary 28.
A.
discĭpŭlus, i, m. 2.   a pupil, scholar.
mūrus, i, m. 2.   a wall.
nāvis, is, f. 3.   a ship.
porta, ae, f. 1.   a gate.

Note.—The Numerals are given on p. 13.

Vocabulary 29.
A.
ĕlĕphantus, i, m. 2.   an elephant.
nauta, ae, m. 1.   a sailor.

B.
māter, tris, f. 3.   a mother.
păter, tris, m. 3.   a father.

Vocabulary 30.
A.
ambŭlo, āvi, ātum, āre, 1.   I walk.
pugno, āvi, ātum, āre, 1.   I fight.
regno, āvi, ātum, āre, 1.   I reign.
salto, āvi, ātum, āre, 1.   I dance.
vĭgĭlo, āvi, ātum, āre, 1.   I watch.
vŏlo, āvi, ātum, āre, 1.   I fly.

VOCABULARIES.

B.

aedĭfĭco, āvi, ātum, āre, 1. *I build.*
ămo, āvi, ātum, āre, 1. *I love.*
expugno, āvi, ātum, āre, 1. *I take by storm.*
firmo, āvi, ātum, āre, 1. *I strengthen.*
intro, āvi, ātum, āre, 1. *I enter.*
laudo, āvi, ātum, āre, 1. *I praise.*
orno, āvi, ātum, āre, 1. *I adorn.*
vĭtŭpĕro, āvi, ātum, āre, 1. *I blame, find-fault-with.*

Vocabulary 31.
B.

oppugno, āvi, ātum, āre, 1. *I attack, assault.*
păro, āvi, ātum, āre, 1. *I prepare, get, gain.*

laus, laudis, *f.* 3. *praise.*

Vocabulary 32.
A.

flōrĕo, flōrŭi, ēre, 2. *I bloom, flourish.*
fulgĕo, fulsi, fulsum, ēre, 2. *I shine, glitter.*
mănĕo, mansi, mansum, ēre, 2. *I remain.*
sĕdĕo, sēdi, sessum, ēre, 2. *I sit.*
tăcĕo, tăcŭi, tăcĭ-tum, ēre, 2. *I am-silent.*
vălĕo, vălŭi, vălĭ-tum, ēre, 2. *I am-in-good-health.*

B.

cŏercĕo, ŭi, ĭtum, ēre, 2. *I restrain, curb.*
dēlĕo, ēvi, ētum, ēre, 2. *I destroy.*

LAT. FOR BEG. I.

dŏcĕo, dŏcŭi, doc-tum, ēre, 2. *I teach.*
hăbĕo, ŭi, ĭtum, ēre, 2. *I have, own, possess.*
mŏnĕo, ŭi, ĭtum, ēre, 2. *I advise, warn.*
tĕnĕo, ŭi, tentum, ēre, 2. *I hold, retain.*
terrĕo, ŭi, ĭtum, ēre, 2. *I terrify, frighten, alarm.*

Vocabulary 33.
B.

mŏvĕo, mōvi, mō-tum, ēre, 2. *I move, disturb.*

Vocabulary 34.
A.

ĕdo, ēdi, ēsum, ĕre, 3. *I eat.*
flŭo, fluxi, flux-um, ĕre, 3. *I flow.*
lūdo, lūsi, lūsum, ĕre, 3. *I play.*
pingo, pinxi, pic-tum, ĕre, 3. *I paint.*
rĕgo, rexi, rec-tum, ĕre, 3. *I rule.*
scrībo, scripsi, scriptum, ĕre, 3. *I write.*

B.

cingo, cinxi, cinc-tum, ĕre, 3. *I surround.*
cŏlo, cŏlŭi, cul-tum, ĕre, 3. *I cultivate.*
dūco, duxi, duc-tum, ĕre, 3. *I lead.*
ĕmo, ēmi, emp-tum, ĕre, 3. *I buy.*
instrŭo, xi, ctum, ĕre, 3. *I arrange, draw-up-in-order.*
pĕto, īvi and ĭi, ītum, ĕre, 3. *I seek.*
tĕgo, texi, tectum, ĕre, 3. *I cover.*
vinco, vīci, vic-tum, ĕre, 3. *I conquer.*

I

Vocabulary 35.

B.

dēfendo, dēfendi, dēfensum, ĕre, 3. *I defend.*
trăho, traxi, tractum, ĕre, 3. *I draw, drag.*

Vocabulary 36.

A.

audĭo, audīvi, audītum, īre, 4. *I hear.*
dormĭo, dormīvi, dormītum, īre, 4. *I sleep.*
ēvĕnĭo, evēni, eventum, īre, 4. *I happen.*
vĕnĭo, vēni, ventum, īre, 4. *I come.*

B.

custōdĭo, īvi, ītum, īre, 4. *I guard, keep-guard.*
ērŭdĭo, īvi, ītum, īre, 4. *I train up, educate.*
mūnĭo, īvi, ītum, īre, 4. *I fortify.*
nŭtrĭo, īvi, ītum, īre, 4. *I nourish, nurture.*
pūnĭo, īvi, ītum, īre, 4. *I punish.*
rĕpĕrĭo, pĕri, pertum, īre, 4. *I find.*
sĕpĕlĭo, īvi *and* ĭi, pultum, īre, 4. *I bury.*

ĕquĕs, ĭtis, *m.* 3. *a horse-soldier.*
pĕdĕs, ĭtis, *m.* *a foot-soldier.*

Vocabulary 37.

B.

fīnĭo, īvi, ītum, īre, 4. *I limit, put-an-end-to.*
scĭo, īvi, ītum, īre, 4. *I know.*
vestĭo, īvi, ītum, īre, 4. *I clothe.*
vincĭo, vinxi, vinctum, īre, 4. *I bind.*

INDEX I. TO VOCABULARIES.
LATIN WORDS.

LIST OF ABBREVIATIONS.

adj.	=	adjective.	m.	=	masculine.
c. or com.	=	common gender.	n.	=	neuter.
f.	=	feminine.	poss. pron.	=	possessive pronoun.
indecl.	=	indeclinable.	pron.	=	pronoun, pronominal.

1, 2, 3, 4, 5, indicate either the *declension* of a noun or the *conjugation* of a verb.

ACIES.

A

ăcĭēs, ēī, *f.*, 5, *a line of battle.*
ăcus, ūs, *f.*, 4, *a needle.*
ăcūtus, a, um, *adj.*, *sharp.*
aedĭfĭco, āvi, ātum, āre, 1, *I build.*
aeger, gra, grum, *adj., sick.*
ăger, ăgri, *m.*, 2, *a field, land.*
āla, ae, *f.*, 1, *a wing.*
albus, a, um, *adj., white.*
altus, a, um, *adj.*, *high, deep.*
ambŭlo, āvi, ātum, āre, 1, *I walk.*
ămīcus, i, *m.*, 2, *a friend.*
ămo, āvi, ātum, āre, 1, *I love.*
angustus, a, um, *adj.*, *narrow.*
ănĭmăl, ālis, *n.*, 3, *an animal.*
antīquus, a, um, *adj., ancient.*
arcus, ūs, *m.*, 4, *a bow.*
arx, arcis, *f.*, 3, *a citadel.*
asper, ĕra, ĕrum, *adj.*, *rough, rugged.*
atrox, ōcis, *adj.*, *stern, sanguinary, cruel.*
audax, ācis, *adj., bold.*
audĭo, īvi, ītum, īre, 4, *I hear.*
aurĕus, a, um, *adj., golden.*
auris, is, *f.*, 3, *an ear.*
aurum, i, *n.*, 2, *gold.*
ăvis, is, *f.*, 3, *a bird.*
ăvus, i, *m.*, 2, *a grandfather.*

CRUS.

B

bellĭcōsus, a, um, *adj., warlike.*
bellum, i, *n.*, 2, *war.*
bĕnignus, a, um, *adj., kind.*
bŏnus, a, um, *adj., good.*
brĕvis, e, *adj., short.*

C

cădo, cĕcĭdi, căsum, ĕre, 3, *I fall.*
caecus, a, um, *adj., blind.*
cănis, is, *com.*, 3, *a dog.*
canto, āvi, ātum, āre, 1, *I sing.*
căpŭt, ĭtis, *n.*, 3, *a head.*
carmĕn, ĭnis, *n.*, 3, *a song.*
cingo, cinxi, cinctum, ĕre, 3, *I surround.*
cīvīlis, e, *adj., belonging to a citizen, civil.*
cīvis, is, *com.*, 3, *a citizen.*
clārus, a, um, *adj., clear, renowned.*
classis, is, *f.*, 3, *a fleet.*
cŏercĕo, ŭi, ĭtum, ēre, 2, *I restrain, curb.*
cōlo, cōlŭi, cultum, ĕre, 3, *I cultivate.*
cŏlōnĭa, ae, *f.*, 1, *a colony.*
cŏlumba, ae, *f.*, 1, *a dove.*
cornu, ūs, *n.*, 4, *a horn.*
cŏrōna, ae, *f.*, 1, *a crown.*
corpus, ŏris, *n.*, 3, *a body.*
crūdēlis, e, *adj., cruel.*
crūs, crūris, *n.*, 3, *a leg.*

DUX.

curro, cŭcurri, cursum, ĕre, 3, *I run.*
currus, ūs, *m.*, 4, *a chariot.*
cursus, ūs, *m.*, 4, *running.*
custōdĭo, īvi, ītum, īre, 4, *I guard, keep-guard.*
custos, custōdis, *com.*, 3, *a guardian.*

D

dēbĭlis, e, *adj., feeble, weak.*
dĕcus, ŏris, *n.*, 3, *an ornament.*
dēfendo, di, sum, ĕre, 3, *I defend.*
dēlĕo, ēvī, ētum, ēre, 2, *I destroy.*
dĭēs, ēī, *m.* and *f.*, 5, *day.*
diffĭcĭlis, e, *adj., difficult.*
dīlĭgens, entis, *adj., diligent, careful.*
discĭpŭlus, i, *m.*, *a pupil, scholar.*
dīvĕs, ĭtis, *adj., rich.*
dŏcĕo, ŭi, ctum, ēre, 2, *I teach.*
doctus, a, um, *adj., learned.*
dŏmĭnus, i, *m.*, 2, *a lord, master.*
dōnum, i, *n.*, 2, *a gift.*
dormĭo, īvi, ītum, īre, 4, *I sleep.*
dūco, duxi, ductum, ĕre, 3, *I lead.*
dulcis, e, *adj., sweet, pleasant (to the taste).*
dux, dŭcis, *com.*, 3, *a leader, general.*

EDO.

E

ĕdo, ēdi, ēsum, ĕre, 3, *I eat*.
effĭgĭēs, ēi, *f.*, 5, *a likeness*.
ēlĕgans, antis, *adj.*, *elegant, exquisite*.
ĕlĕphantus, i, *m.*, 2, *an elephant*.
ĕmo, ēmi, emptum, ĕre, 3, *I buy*.
ĕquĕs, ĭtis, *m.*, 3, *a horse-soldier*.
ĕquĭtātus, ūs, *m.*, 4, *cavalry*.
ĕquus, i, *m.*, 2, *a horse*.
ērŭdĭo, īvi, ītum, īre, 4, *I train up, educate*.
ēvĕnĭo, vēni, ventum, īre, 4, *I happen*.
exercĭtus, ūs, *m.*, 4, *an army*.
expugno, āvi, ātum, āre, 1, *I take by storm*.

F

făcĭēs, ēi, *f.*, 5, *countenance, face*.
fămēs, is, *f.*, 3, *hunger*.
fēlix, īcis, *adj.*, *happy, fortunate, fruitful*.
fēmĭna, ae, *f.*, 1, *a woman*.
fĕrox, ōcis, *adj.*, *fierce, spirited*.
fīcus, ūs, *f.*, 4, *a fig*.
fĭdēlis, e, *adj., faithful*.
fĭdēs, ēi, *f.*, 5, *faith, fidelity*.
fīlĭa, ae, *f.*, 1, *a daughter*.
fīlĭus, i, *m.*, 2, *a son*.
fīnĭo, īvi, ītum, īre, 4, *I limit, put an end to*.
firmo, āvi, ātum, āre, 1, *I strengthen*.
firmus, a, um, *adj., strong*.
flōrens, ntis, *adj., flourishing*.
flōrĕo, ŭi, ēre, 2, *I bloom, flourish*.
flŭo, fluxi, fluxum, ĕre, 3, *I flow*.
flŭvĭus, ii, *m.*, 2, *a river*.
fortis, e, *adj., strong, brave*.
fulgĕo, fulsi, fulsum, ēre, 2, *I shine, glitter*.

G

gĕner, ĕri, *m.*, 2, *a son-in-law*.
glădĭus, ii, *m.*, 2, *a sword*.
grăcĭlis, e, *adj., thin, slender*.
grāmen, ĭnis, *n.*, 3, *grass*.
grăvis, e, *adj., heavy, severe*.

MAGISTRATUS.

H

hăbĕo, ŭi, ĭtum, ēre, 2, *I have, own, possess*.
hĭlăris, e, *adj., cheerful*.
hortus, i, *m.*, 2, *a garden*.
hostis, is, *com.*, 3, *an enemy*.
hŭmĭlis, e, *adj., low*.

I

imprŏbus, a, um, *adj., wicked*.
indoctus, a, um, *adj., unlearned*.
iners, tis, *adj., helpless, sluggish*.
ingens, entis, *adj., immense*.
ĭnĭmīcus, i, *m.*, 2, *an enemy*.
injustus, a, um, *adj., unjust*.
innŭmĕrus, a, um, *adj., innumerable*.
instrŭo, xi, ctum, ĕre, 3, *I arrange, draw up in order*.
insŭla, ae, *f.*, 1, *an island*.
intro, āvi, ātum, āre, 1, *I enter*.

J

jūcundus, a, um, *adj., pleasant*.
jūdex, ĭcis, *com.*, 3, *a judge*.
justus, a, um, *adj., just*.

L

lăcus, ūs, *m.*, 4, *a lake*.
laetus, a, um, *adj., joyful*.
lātus, a, um, *adj., wide, broad*.
laudo, āvi, ātum, āre, 1, *I praise*.
laus, laudis, *f.*, 3, *praise*.
lĕvis, e, *adj., light (not heavy)*.
lex, lēgis, *f.*, 3, *a law*.
līber, libri, *m.*, 2, *a book*.
līber, ĕra, ĕrum, *adj., free*.
lītus, ŏris, *n.*, 3, *a shore*.
longus, a, um, *adj., long*.
lūdus, i, *m.*, 2, *play, game*.
lūdo, lūsi, lūsum, ĕre, 3, *I play*.

M

măgister, tri, *m.*, 2, *a master, teacher*.
măgistrātus, ūs, *m.*, 4, *a magistrate*.

ORNO.

magnus, a, um, *adj., great, large*.
mălus, a, um, *adj., bad, wicked*.
mănĕo, mansi, mansum, ēre, 2, *I remain*.
mănus, ūs, *f.*, 4, *a hand*.
măre, is, *n.*, 3, *the sea*.
māter, tris, *f.*, 3, *a mother*.
mĕmŏrābĭlis, e, *adj., to be remembered, memorable*.
mendax, ācis, *adj., lying, false*.
mĕrīdĭēs, ēi, *m.*, 5, *midday, noon*.
mīlĕs, mīlĭtis, *m.*, 3, *a soldier*.
mĭnister, tri, *m.*, 2, *a servant*.
mītis, e, *adj., mild*.
mŏlestus, a, um, *adj., troublesome*.
mollis, e, *adj., soft, mellow*.
mŏnĕo, ŭi, ĭtum, ēre, 2, *I advise, warn*.
mŏvĕo, mōvi, mōtum, ēre, 2, *I move, disturb*.
multus, a, um, *adj., much, many*.
mūnĭo, īvi, ītum, īre, 4, *I fortify*.
mūrus, i, *m.*, 2, *a wall*.

N

nauta, ae, *m.*, 1, *a sailor*.
nāvālis, e, *adj., naval*.
nāvis, is, *f.*, 3, *a ship*.
nĭger, gra, grum, *adj., black*.
nōbĭlis, e, *adj., distinguished*.
nōmen, ĭnis, *n.*, 3, *a name*.
noster, tra, trum, *poss. pron., our*.
nŏvus, a, um, *adj., new*.
nūtrĭo, īvi, ītum, īre, 4, *I nourish, nurture*.

O

obsĕs, ĭdis, *com.*, 3, *a hostage*.
occīdo, īdi, īsum, ĕre, 3, *I slay, kill*.
omnis, e, *adj., all, every, whole*.
oppĭdum, i, *n.*, 2, *a town*.
oppugno, āvi, ātum, āre, 1, *I attack, assault*.
orno, āvi, ātum, āre, 1, *I adorn*.

INDEX TO VOCABULARIES.—LATIN WORDS.

P

păro, āvi, ātum, āre, 1, *I prepare, obtain.*
parvus, a, um, *adj., small, little.*
păter, tris, *m.,* 3, *a father.*
paucus, a, um, *adj., few.*
pĕdĕs, ĭtis, *m.,* 3, *a foot-soldier.*
pĕdĭtātus, ūs, *m.,* 4, *infantry.*
pĕrīcŭlum, i, *n.,* 2, *danger.*
pĕrītus, a, um, *adj., skilful.*
perniciēs, ēi, *f.,* 5, *destruction, ruin.*
perniciōsus, a, um, *adj., destructive.*
pĕto, īvi and ĭi, ītum, ĕre, 3, *I seek.*
pingo, pinxi, pictum, ĕre, 3, *I paint.*
plānĭtĭēs, ēi, *f.,* 5, *a plain.*
porta, ae, *f.,* 1, *a gate.*
portus, ūs, *m.,* 4, *a harbour.*
pŏtens, entis, *adj., powerful.*
praemĭum, ii, *n.,* 2, *a reward.*
praestans, antis, *adj., excellent.*
proelĭum, ii, *n.,* 2, *a battle.*
prūdens, entis, *adj., prudent.*
pŭella, ae, *f.,* 1, *a girl.*
pŭer, ĕri, *m.,* 2, *a boy.*
pugno, āvi, ātum, āre, 1, *I fight.*
pulcher, chra, chrum, *adj., beautiful.*
pūnĭo, īvi, ītum, ire, 4, *I punish.*
pŭto, āvi, ātum, āre, 1, *I think.*

Q

quĕrcus, ūs, *f.,* 4, *an oak.*

R

răpax, ācis, *adj., rapacious.*
răpĭdus, a, um, *adj., rapid.*
rārus, a, um, *adj., rare.*
rēgīna, ae, *f.,* 1, *a queen.*
regno, āvi, ātum, āre, 1, *I reign.*
regnum, i, *n.,* 2, *a kingdom.*
rĕgo, rexi, rectum, ĕre, 3, *I rule.*
rĕpĕrĭo, pĕri, pertum, ire, 4, *I find.*
rēs, rĕi, *f.,* 5, *a thing.*
rēte, is, *n.,* 3, *a net.*
rex, rēgis, *m.,* 3, *a king.*
rŏsa, ae, *f.,* 1, *a rose.*
rūpēs, is, *f.,* 3, *a rock.*

S

săcer, cra, crum, *adj., sacred.*
săgitta, ae, *f.,* 1, *an arrow.*
salto, āvi, ātum, āre, 1, *I dance.*
săpĭens, entis, *adj., wise.*
scĭo, īvi, ītum, ire, 4, *I know.*
scrībo, psi, ptum, ĕre, 3, *I write.*
scūtum, i, *n.,* 2, *a shield.*
sĕdĕo, sēdi, sessum, ĕre, 2, *I sit.*
segnĭtĭēs, ēi, *f.,* 5, *slothfulness, indolence.*
sĕpĕllo, īvi and ĭi, ītum, ire, 4, *I bury.*
sĕrēnus, a, um, *adj., clear, calm.*
servus, i, *m.,* 2, *a slave.*
sĕvērus, a, um, *adj., severe.*
sīdus, ĕris, *n.,* 3, *a star, constellation.*
sĭmĭlis, e, *adj., like.*
sŏcer, ĕri, *m.,* 2, *a father-in-law.*
spēs, ēi, *f.,* 5, *hope.*
splendĭdus, a, um, *adj., splendid, bright.*
suāvis, e, *adj., sweet (to the smell), delightful.*

T

tăcĕo, ŭi, ĭtum, ĕre, 2, *I am silent.*
tālis, e, *adj., of that sort, such.*
tĕgo, texi, tectum, ĕre, 3, *I cover.*
templum, i, *n.,* 2, *a temple.*
tĕnĕo, ŭi, tentum, ĕre, 2, *I hold, retain.*
tĕner, ĕra, ĕrum, *adj., tender, soft.*
tĕnŭis, e, *adj., thin, delicate, slender.*
terrĕo, ŭi, ĭtum, ĕre, 2, *I terrify, frighten, alarm.*
tĭmĭdus, a, um, *adj., timid.*
trabs, trăbis, *f.,* 3, *a beam.*
trăho, traxi, tractum, ĕre, 3, *I draw, drag.*
tristis, e, *adj., sad, sorrowful.*
turpis, e, *adj., base, disgraceful.*
turris, is, *f.,* 3, *a tower.*
tūtus, a, um, *adj., safe.*

U

urbs, urbis, *f.,* 3, *a city.*
ūtĭlis, e, *adj., useful.*

V

vălĕo, ŭi, ĭtum, ĕre, 2, *I am strong, in good health.*
vălĭdus, a, um, *adj., strong.*
vallis, is, *f.,* 3, *a valley.*
vărĭus, a, um, *adj., different, various.*
vēlox, ōcis, *adj., swift.*
vĕnĭo, vēni, ventum, ire, 4, *I come.*
vester, tra, trum, *poss. pron., your.*
vestĭo, īvi, ītum, ire, 4, *I clothe.*
vĭgĭlo, āvi, ātum, āre, 1, *I watch.*
vīlis, e, *adj., cheap, common.*
vincĭo, vinxi, vinctum, ire, 4, *I bind.*
vinco, vici, victum, ĕre, 3, *I conquer.*
vĭtŭpĕro, āvi, ātum, āre, 1, *I blame, find fault with.*
vŏlo, āvi, ātum, āre, 1, *I fly.*

INDEX II. TO VOCABULARIES.

ENGLISH WORDS.

A

adorn, orno, āvi, ātum, ēre, 1.
advise, mŏnĕo, ŭi, ĭtum, ēre, 2.
alarm, terrĕo, ŭi, ĭtum, ēre, 2.
all, omnis, e, *adj.*
ancient, antiquus, a, um, *adj.*
animal, ănĭmăl, ālis, *n.*, 3.
army, exercĭtus, ūs, *m.*, 4.
arrange, instrŭo, xi, ctum, ēre, 3.
assault, attack, oppugno, āvi, ātum, āre, 1.
attentive, attentus, a, um, *adj.*

B

bad, mălus, a, um, *adj.*
base, turpis, e, *adj.*
battle, proelĭum, ii, *n.*, 2.
beam, trabs, trăbis, *f.*, 3.
beautiful, pulcher, chra, chrum, *adj.*
bind, vincĭo, vinxi, vinctum, īre, 4.
bird, ăvis, is, *f.*, 3.
black, nĭger, gra, grum, *adj.*
blame, vĭtŭpĕro, āvi, ātum, āre, 1.
blind, caecus, a, um, *adj.*
bloom, flŏrĕo, ŭi, ēre, 2.
body, corpus, ŏris, *n.*, 3.
bold, audax, ācis, *adj.*
book, lĭber, bri, *m.*, 2.
bow, arcus, ūs, *m.*, 4.
boy, pŭer, ĕri, *m.*, 2.
brave, fortis, e, *adj.*
bright, splendĭdus, a, um, *adj.*
broad, lātus, a, um, *adj.*
build, aedĭfĭco, āvi, ātum, āre, 1.
bury, sepelĭo, īvi *and* ĭi, pultum, īre, 4.
buy, ĕmo, ēmi, emptum, ĕre, 3.

C

calm, sĕrēnus, a, um, *adj.*
careful, dīlĭgens, entis, *adj.*
cavalry, ĕquĭtātus, ūs, *m.*, 4.
chariot, currus, ūs, *m.*, 4.
cheap, vīlis, e, *adj.*
cheerful, hĭlăris, e, *adj.*
citadel, arx, arcis, *f.*, 3.
citizen, cīvis, is, *c.*, 3.
city, urbs, urbis, *f.*, 3.
civil, cīvīlis, e, *adj.*
clear, clārus, a, um, *adj.*; sĕrēnus, a, um, *adj.*
clothe, vestĭo, īvi, ītum, īre, 4.
colony, cŏlōnĭa, ae, *f.*, 1.
come, vĕnĭo, vēni, ventum, īre, 4.
common, vīlis, e, *adj.*
conquer, vinco, vīci, victum, ĕre, 3.
countenance, făcĭēs, ēi, *f.*, 5.
cover, tĕgo, texi, tectum, ĕre, 3.
crown, cŏrōna, ae, *f.*, 1.
cruel, crūdēlis, e, *adj.*
——— (*stern, sanguinary*), atrox, ōcis, *adj.*
cultivate, cŏlo, cŏlŭi, cultum, ĕre, 3.
curb, cŏercĕo, ŭi, ĭtum, ēre, 2.

D

dance, salto, āvi, ātum, āre, 1.
danger, pĕrīcŭlum, i, *n.*, 2.
daughter, fīlĭa, ae, *f.*, 1.
day, dĭēs, ēi, *m.* and *f.*, 5.
deep, altus, a, um, *adj.*
defend, dēfendo, di, sum, ĕre, 3.
delicate, tĕnŭis, e, *adj.*
delightful, suāvis, e, *adj.*
destroy, dēlĕo, ēvi, ētum, ēre, 2.
destruction, pernĭcĭēs, ēi, *f.*, 5.
destructive, pernĭcĭōsus, a, um, *adj.*
difficult, diffĭcĭlis, e, *adj.*
diligent, dīlĭgens, entis, *adj.*
disgraceful, turpis, e, *adj.*
distinguished, nōbĭlis, e, *adj.*
disturb, mŏvĕo, mōvi, mōtum, ēre, 2.
dog, cănis, is, *c.*, 3.
dove, cŏlumba, ae, *f.*, 1.
drag, draw, trăho, traxi, tractum, ĕre, 3.
draw-up-in-order, instrŭo, xi, ctum, ĕre, 3.

E

ear, auris, is, *f.*, 3.
eat, ĕdo, ēdi, ēsum, ĕre, 3.
educate, ērŭdĭo, īvi, ītum, īre, 4.
elegant, ēlĕgans, antis, *adj.*
elephant, ĕlĕphantus, i, *m.*, 2.
enemy (*public*), hostis, is, *c.*, 3.
enemy (*personal*), ĭnĭmīcus, i, *m.*, 2.
enter, intro, āvi, ātum, āre, 1.
every, omnis, e, *adj.*
excellent, praestans, antis, *adj.*
exquisite, ēlĕgans, antis, *adj.*

F

face, făcĭēs, ēi, *f.*, 5.
faith, fĭdēs, ēi, *f.*, 5.
faithful, fĭdēlis, e, *adj.*
fall, cădo, cĕcĭdi, cāsum, ĕre, 3.
false, mendax, ācis, *adj.*
father, păter, tris, *m.*, 3.
father-in-law, sŏcer, ĕri, *m.*, 2.
feeble, dēbĭlis, e, *adj.*
few, paucus, a, um, *adj.*
fidelity, fĭdēs, ēi, *f.*, 5.
field, ăger, gri, *m.*, 2.
fierce, fĕrox, ōcis, *adj.*
fig, fīcus, ūs, *f.*, 4.
fight, pugno, āvi, ātum, āre, 1.
find, rĕpĕrĭo, pĕri, pertum, īre, 4.

INDEX TO VOCABULARIES.—ENGLISH WORDS. 103

FIND-FAULT-WITH.

find-fault-with, vĭtŭpĕro, āvī, ātum, āre, 1.
fleet, classis, is, *f.*, 3.
flourish, flōrĕo, ŭī, ēre, 2.
flourishing, flōrens, entis, *adj.*
flow, flŭo, fluxī, fluxum, ēre, 3.
fly, vŏlo, āvī, ātum, āre, 1.
foot-soldier, pĕdĕs, ĭtis, *m.*, 3.
fortify, mūnĭo, īvī, ītum, īre, 4.
fortunate, fēlix, īcis, *adj.*
free, līber, ĕra, ĕrum, *adj.*
friend, ămīcus, ī, *m.*, 2.
frighten, terrĕo, ŭī, ĭtum, ēre, 2.
fruitful, fēlix, īcis, *adj.*

G

gain, păro, āvī, ātum, āre, 1.
garden, hortus, ī, *m.*, 2.
gate, porta, ae, *f.*, 1.
general, dux, dŭcis, *c.*, 3.
gentle, mītis, e, *adj.*
get, păro, āvī, ātum, āre, 1.
gift, dōnum, ī, *n.*, 2.
girl, pŭella, ae, *f.*, 1.
glitter, fulgĕo, fulsī, fulsum, ēre, 2.
gold, aurum, ī, *n.*, 2.
golden, aurĕus, a, um, *adj.*
good, bŏnus, a, um, *adj.*
grandfather, ăvus, ī, *m.*, 2.
grass, grāmen, ĭnis, *n.*, 3.
great, magnus, a, um, *adj.*
guard, custōdĭo, īvī, ītum, īre, 4.
guardian, custos, ōdis, *c.*, 3.

H

hand, mănus, ūs, *f.*, 4.
happen, ēvĕnĭo, vēnī, ventum, īre, 4.
happy, fēlix, īcis, *adj.*
harbour, portus, ūs, *m.*, 4.
have, hăbĕo, ŭī, ĭtum, ēre, 2.
head, căpŭt, ĭtis, *n.*, 3.
health, be in, vălĕo, ŭī, ĭtum, ēre, 2.
hear, audĭo, īvī, ītum, īre, 4.
heavy, grăvis, e, *adj.*
helpless, iners, tis, *adj.*
high, altus, a, um, *adj.*
hold, tĕnĕo, ŭī, tentum, ēre, 2.
hope, spēs, ĕī, *f.*, 5.
horn, cornu, ūs, *n.*, 4.

LYING.

horse, ĕquus, ī, *m.*, 2.
horse-soldier, ĕquĕs, ĭtis, *m.*, 3.
hostage, obsĕs, ĭdis, *c.*, 3.
hunger, fămēs, is, *f.*, 3.

I

immense, ingens, tis, *adj.*
indolence, segnĭtĭēs, ēī, *f.*, 5.
infantry, pĕdĭtātus, ūs, *m.*, 4.
innumerable, innŭmĕrus, a, um, *adj.*
island, insŭla, ae, *f.*, 1.

J

joyful, laetus, a, um, *adj.*
judge, jūdex, jūdĭcis, *c.*, 3.
just, justus, a, um, *adj.*

K

keep-guard, custōdĭo, īvī, ĭtum, īre, 4.
kill, occīdo, cīdī, cīsum, ĕre, 3.
kind, bĕnignus, a, um, *adj.*
king, rex, rēgis, *m.*, 3.
kingdom, regnum, ī, *n.*, 2.
know, scĭo, īvī, ĭtum, īre, 4.

L

lake, lăcus, ūs, *m.*, 4.
land, ăger, grī, *m.*, 2.
large, magnus, a, um, *adj.*
law, lex, lēgis, *f.*, 3.
lead, dūco, duxī, ductum, ĕre, 3.
leader, dux, dŭcis, *c.*, 3.
learned, doctus, a, um, *adj.*
leg, crūs, crūris, *n.*, 3.
light (*not heavy*), lĕvis, e, *adj.*
like (*adj.*), sĭmĭlis, e, *adj.*
likeness, effĭgĭēs, ēī, *f.*, 5.
limit, fīnĭo, īvī, ītum, īre, 4.
line-of-battle, ăcĭēs, ēī, *f.*, 5.
little, parvus, a, um, *adj.*
long, longus, a, um, *adj.*
lord, dŏmĭnus, ī, *m.*, 2.
love, ămo, āvī, ātum, āre, 1.
low, hŭmĭlis, e, *adj.*
lying, mendax, ācis, *adj.*

PUT-AN-END-TO.

M

magistrate, măgistrātus, ūs, *m.*, 4.
many, multus, a, um, *adj.*
master (*teacher*), măgister, trī, *m.*, 2.
master (*lord*), dŏmĭnus, ī, *m.*, 2.
mellow, mollis, e, *adj.*
memorable, mĕmŏrābĭlis, e, *adj.*
mid-day, mĕrīdĭēs, ēī, *m.*, 5.
mild, mītis, e, *adj.*
mother, māter, tris, *f.*, 3.
move, mŏvĕo, mōvī, mōtum, ēre, 2.
much, multus, a, um, *adj.*

N

name, nōmen, ĭnis, *n.*, 3.
narrow, angustus, a, um, *adj.*
naval, nāvālis, e, *adj.*
needle, ăcus, ūs, *f.*, 4.
net, rēte, is, *n.*, 3.
new, nŏvus, a, um, *adj.*
noon, mĕrīdĭēs, ēī, *m.*, 5.
nourish, nurture, nūtrĭo, īvī, ītum, īre, 4.

O

oak, quercus, ūs, *f.*, 4.
ornament, dĕcus, ŏris, *n.*, 3.
our, noster, tra, trum, *poss.* [*pron.*]
own, hăbĕo, ŭī, ĭtum, ēre, 2.

P

paint, pingo, pinxī, pictum, ĕre, 3.
plain, plānĭtĭēs, ēī, *f.*, 5.
play, lūdo, lūsī, lūsum, ĕre, 3.
pleasant, jūcundus, a, um, *adj.*
powerful, pŏtens, entis, *adj.*
possess, hăbĕo, ŭī, ĭtum, ēre, 2.
praise, laus, dis, *f.*, 3.
praise (to), laudo, āvī, ātum, āre, 1.
prepare, păro, āvī, ātum, āre, 1.
prudent, prūdens, entis, *adj.*
punish, pūnĭo, īvī, ītum, īre, 4.
pupil, discĭpŭlus, ī, *m.*, 2.
put-an-end-to, fīnĭo, īvī, ĭtum, īre, 4.

Q

queen, rēgīna, ae, *f.*, 1.

R

rapacious, răpax, ācis, *adj.*
rapid, răpĭdus, a, um, *adj.*
rare, rārus, a, um, *adj.*
reign, regno, āvi, ātum, āre, 1.
remain, mănĕo, mansi, mansum, ēre, 2.
renowned, clārus, a, um, *adj.*
restrain, cŏercĕo, ŭi, ĭtum, ēre, 2.
retain, tĕnĕo, ŭi, tentum, ēre, 2.
reward, praemĭum, ii, *n.*, 2.
rich, dīves, ĭtis, *adj.*
river, flŭvĭus, ii, *m.*, 2.
rock, rūpēs, is, *f.*, 3.
rose, rŏsa, ae, *f.*, 1.
rough, rugged, asper, ĕra, ĕrum, *adj.*
ruin, pernĭcĭēs, ēi, *f.*, 5.
rule, rĕgo, rexi, rectum, ēre, 3.
run, curro, cŭcurri, cursum, ēre, 3.
running, cursus, ūs, *m.*, 4.

S

sacred, săcer, cra, crum, *adj.*
sad, tristis, e, *adj.* [*adj.*
safe, tūtus, a, um, *adj.*
sailor, nauta, ae, *m.*, 1.
sanguinary, atrox, ōcis, *adj.*
scholar, discĭpŭlus, i, *m.*, 2.
sea, măre, is, *n.*, 3.
seek, pĕto, īvi *and* ĭi, ītum, ēre, 3. [2.
servant, mĭnister, tri, *m.*,
severe, grăvis, e, *adj.*; sĕvērus, a, um, *adj.*
sharp, ăcūtus, a, um, *adj.*
shield, scūtum, i, *n.*, 2.
shine, fulgĕo, fulsi, fulsum, ēre, 2.
ship, nāvis, is, *f.*, 3.
shore, lītus, ōris, *n.*, 3.
short, brĕvis, e, *adj.*
sick, aeger, gra, grum, *adj.*
silent, be, tăcĕo, ŭi, ĭtum, ēre, 2.
sing, canto, āvi, ātum, āre, 1. [2.
sit, sĕdĕo, sēdi, sessum, ēre,
skilful, pĕrītus, a, um, *adj.*
slave, servus, i, *m.*, 2.
sleep, dormĭo, īvi, ītum, īre, 4.
slender, grăcĭlis, e, *adj.*; tĕnŭis, e, *adj.*
slothfulness, segnĭtĭēs, ēi, *f.*, 5.
sluggish, iners, ertis, *adj.*
small, parvus, a, um, *adj.*
soft, mollis, e, *adj.*
soldier, mīlĕs, mīlĭtis, *m.*,
son, fīlĭus, i, *m.*, 2. [3.
song, carmen, ĭnis, *n.*, 3.
son-in-law, gĕner, ĕri, *m.*, 2.
sorrowful, tristis, e, *adj.*
spirited, fĕrox, ōcis, *adj.*
splendid, splendĭdus, a, um, *adj.*
star, sīdus, ĕris, *n.*, 3.
stern, atrox, ōcis, *adj.*
strengthen, firmo, āvi, ātum, āre, 1.
strong (*from position, firm, immovable*), firmus, a, um, *adj.*
strong (*because brave*), fortis, e, *adj.*
strong (*able to perform*), vălĭdus, a, um, *adj.*
successful, fēlix, īcis, *adj.*
such, tālis, e, *adj.*
surround, cingo, cinxi, cinctum, ĕre, 3.
sweet (*to the smell*), suāvis, e, *adj.*
sweet (*to the taste*), dulcis, e, *adj.*
swift, vēlox, ōcis, *adj.*
sword, glădĭus, ii, *m.*, 2.

T

take-by-storm, expugno, āvi, ātum, āre, 1.
teach, dŏcĕo, dŏcŭi, doctum, ēre, 2.
teacher, măgister, tri, *m.*, 2.
temple, templum, i, *n.*, 2.
tender, tĕner, ĕra, ĕrum, *adj.*
terrify, terrĕo, ŭi, ĭtum, ēre, 2.
thin (*slender*), grăcĭlis, e, *adj.*; tĕnŭis, e, *adj.* (fr. tendo, *to stretch*, lit. *stretched out; hence fine, delicate*).
thing, rēs, rĕi, *f.*, 5.
think, pŭto, āvi, ātum. āre, 1.
timid, tĭmĭdus, a, um, *adj.*
tower, turris, is, *f.*, 3.
town, oppĭdum, i, *n.*, 2.
train-up, ērŭdĭo, īvi, ītum, īre, 4.
troublesome, mŏlestus, a, um, *adj.*

U

unjust, injustus, a, um, *adj.* [um, *adj.*
unlearned, indoctus, a,
useful, ūtĭlis, e, *adj.*

V

valley, vallis, is, *f.*, 3.
various, vărĭus, a, um, *adj.*

W

walk, ambŭlo, āvi, ātum, āre, 1.
wall, mūrus, i, *m.*, 2.
war, bellum, i, *n.*, 2.
warlike, bellĭcōsus, a, um, *adj.*
warn, mŏnĕo, ŭi, ĭtum, ēre,
watch, vĭgĭlo, āvi, ātum, āre, 1.
weak, dēbĭlis, e, *adj.*
white, albus, a, um, *adj.*
whole, omnis, e, *adj.*
wicked, imprŏbus, a, um, *adj.*
wide, lātus, a, um, *adj.*
wing, āla, ae, *f.*, 1.
wise, săpĭens, entis, *adj.*
woman, fēmĭna, ae, *f.*, 1.
write, scrībo, scripsi, scriptum, ĕre, 3.

Y

your, vester, tra, trum, *poss. pron.*

50, Albemarle Street, London,
March, 1879.

MR. MURRAY'S
LIST OF SCHOOL BOOKS.

MURRAY'S STUDENT'S MANUALS:
A Series of Class-books for advanced Scholars.

FORMING A CHAIN OF HISTORY FROM THE EARLIEST AGES
DOWN TO MODERN TIMES.

"We are glad of an opportunity of directing the attention of teachers to these admirable schoolbooks."—*The Museum.*

THE STUDENT'S OLD TESTAMENT HISTORY. From the Creation of the World to the Return of the Jews from Captivity. With an Introduction to the Books of the Old Testament. By PHILIP SMITH, B.A. With 40 Maps and Woodcuts. (630 pp.) Post 8vo. 7s. 6d.

THE STUDENT'S NEW TESTAMENT HISTORY. With an Introduction, containing the connection of the Old and New Testaments. By PHILIP SMITH, B.A. With 30 Maps and Woodcuts. (680 pp.) Post 8vo. 7s. 6d.

THE STUDENT'S MANUAL OF ECCLESIASTICAL HISTORY. From the Times of the Apostles to the Full Establishment of the Holy Roman Empire and the Papal Power. By PHILIP SMITH, B.A. With Woodcuts. Post 8vo. 7s. 6d.

THE STUDENT'S MANUAL OF ENGLISH CHURCH HISTORY. From the Accession of Henry VIIIth to the Silencing of Convocation in the Eighteenth Century. By G. G. PERRY, M.A. Post 8vo. 7s. 6d.

THE STUDENT'S ANCIENT HISTORY OF THE EAST. From the Earliest Times to the Conquests of Alexander the Great, including Egypt, Assyria, Babylonia, Media, Persia, Asia Minor, and Phœnicia. By PHILIP SMITH, B.A. With 70 Woodcuts. (608 pp.) Post 8vo. 7s. 6d.

THE STUDENT'S HISTORY OF GREECE. From the Earliest Times to the Roman Conquest. With Chapters on the History of Literature and Art. By WM. SMITH, D.C.L. With 100 Woodcuts. (640 pp.) Post 8vo. 7s. 6d. *** *Questions on the "Student's Greece."* 12mo. 2s.

THE STUDENT'S HISTORY OF ROME. From the Earliest Times to the Establishment of the Empire. With Chapters on the History of Literature and Art. By DEAN LIDDELL. With 80 Woodcuts. (686 pp.) Post 8vo. 7s. 6d.

THE STUDENT'S GIBBON; An Epitome of the History of the Decline and Fall of the Roman Empire. By EDWARD GIBBON. Incorporating the researches of recent historians. With 200 Woodcuts. (700 pp.) Post 8vo. 7s. 6d.

[*Continued.*

MURRAY'S STUDENT'S MANUALS.

THE STUDENT'S MANUAL OF ANCIENT GEOGRAPHY. By REV. W. L. BEVAN, M.A. With 158 Woodcuts. (710 pp.) Post 8vo. 7s. 6d.

THE STUDENT'S MANUAL OF MODERN GEOGRAPHY, MATHEMATICAL, PHYSICAL, AND DESCRIPTIVE. By REV. W. L. BEVAN, M.A. With 120 Woodcuts. (684 pp.) Post 8vo. 7s. 6d.

THE STUDENT'S HISTORY OF EUROPE DURING THE MIDDLE AGES. By HENRY HALLAM, LL.D. (650 pp.) Post 8vo. 7s. 6d.

THE STUDENT'S CONSTITUTIONAL HISTORY OF ENGLAND. FROM THE ACCESSION OF HENRY VII. TO THE DEATH OF GEORGE II. By HENRY HALLAM, LL.D. (680 pp.) Post 8vo. 7s. 6d.

THE STUDENT'S HUME; A HISTORY OF ENGLAND, FROM THE EARLIEST TIMES TO THE REVOLUTION IN 1688. By DAVID HUME. Incorporating the Corrections and Researches of recent Historians, and continued to 1868. With 70 Woodcuts. (780 pp.) Post 8vo. 7s. 6d.

*** *Questions on the "Student's Hume."* 12mo. 2s.

THE STUDENT'S HISTORY OF FRANCE. FROM THE EARLIEST TIMES TO THE ESTABLISHMENT OF THE SECOND EMPIRE, 1852. With Notes and Illustrations on the Institutions of the Country. By REV. W. H. JERVIS, M.A. With Woodcuts. (724 pp.) Post 8vo. 7s. 6d.

THE STUDENT'S MANUAL OF THE ENGLISH LANGUAGE. By GEORGE P. MARSH. (538 pp.) Post 8vo. 7s. 6d.

THE STUDENT'S MANUAL OF ENGLISH LITERATURE. By T. B. SHAW, M.A. (510 pp.) Post 8vo. 7s. 6d.

THE STUDENT'S SPECIMENS OF ENGLISH LITERATURE. Selected from the BEST WRITERS. By THOS. B. SHAW, M.A. (560 pp.) Post 8vo. 7s. 6d.

THE STUDENT'S ELEMENTS OF GEOLOGY. By SIR CHARLES LYELL, F.R.S. With 600 Woodcuts. (692 pp.) Post 8vo. 9s.

THE STUDENT'S MANUAL OF MORAL PHILOSOPHY. With Quotations and References. By WILLIAM FLEMING, D.D. (440 pp.) Post 8vo. 7s. 6d.

THE STUDENT'S BLACKSTONE. AN ABRIDGMENT OF THE ENTIRE COMMENTARIES. By R. MALCOLM KERR, LL.D. (670 pp.) Post 8vo. 7s. 6d.

THE STUDENT'S EDITION OF AUSTIN'S JURISPRUDENCE. Compiled from the larger work. By ROBERT CAMPBELL. Post 8vo. 12s.

AN ANALYSIS OF AUSTIN'S LECTURES ON JURISPRUDENCE. By GORDON CAMPBELL, of the Inner Temple. Post 8vo. 6s.

DR. WM. SMITH'S SMALLER HISTORIES.

These Works have been drawn up for the lower forms, at the request of several teachers, who require more elementary books than the STUDENT'S HISTORICAL MANUALS.

A SMALLER SCRIPTURE HISTORY OF THE OLD AND NEW TESTAMENTS. Edited by WM. SMITH, D.C.L. With 40 Woodcuts. (370 pp.) 16mo. 3s. 6d.
"Students well know the value of Dr. Wm. Smith's larger Scripture History. This abridgment omits nothing of importance, and is presented in such a handy form that it cannot fail to become a valuable aid to the less learned Bible Student."—*People's Magazine.*

A SMALLER ANCIENT HISTORY OF THE EAST, from the EARLIEST TIMES to the CONQUEST OF ALEXANDER THE GREAT. By PHILIP SMITH, B.A. With 70 Woodcuts. (310 pp.) 16mo. 3s. 6d.
"Designed to aid the study of the Scriptures, by placing in their true historical relations those allusions to Egypt, Assyria, Babylonia, Phœnicia, and the Medo-Persian Empire, which form the background of the history of Israel. The present work is an indispensable adjunct of the 'Smaller Scripture History;' and the two have been written expressly to be used together."—*Preface.*

A SMALLER HISTORY OF GREECE, from the EARLIEST TIMES to the ROMAN CONQUEST. By WM. SMITH, D.C.L. With 74 Woodcuts. (268 pp.) 16mo. 3s. 6d.

A SMALLER HISTORY OF ROME, from the EARLIEST TIMES to the ESTABLISHMENT OF THE EMPIRE. By WM. SMITH, D.C.L. With 70 Woodcuts. (324 pp.) 16mo. 3s. 6d.

A SMALLER CLASSICAL MYTHOLOGY. With Translations from the Ancient Poets, and Questions on the Work. By H. R. LOCKWOOD. With 90 Woodcuts. (300 pp.) 16mo. 3s. 6d.

A SMALLER MANUAL OF ANCIENT GEOGRAPHY. By Rev. W. L. BEVAN, M.A. With 36 Woodcuts. (240 pp.) 16mo. 3s. 6d.

A SCHOOL MANUAL OF MODERN GEOGRAPHY, PHYSICAL and POLITICAL. By REV. JOHN RICHARDSON, M.A. (400 pp.) Post 8vo. 5s.

A SMALLER HISTORY OF ENGLAND. From the EARLIEST TIMES to the year 1868. By PHILIP SMITH, B.A. With 68 Woodcuts. (400 pp.) 16mo. 3s. 6d.

A SMALLER HISTORY OF ENGLISH LITERATURE; giving a sketch of the lives of our chief writers. By JAMES ROWLEY. (276 pp.) 16mo. 3s. 6d.

SHORT SPECIMENS OF ENGLISH LITERATURE. Selected from the chief authors and arranged chronologically. By JAMES ROWLEY. With Notes. (368 pp.) 16mo. 3s. 6d.

DR. WM. SMITH'S DICTIONARIES.

BIBLICAL, CLASSICAL, AND LATIN.

DICTIONARY OF THE BIBLE; Its Antiquities, Biography, Geography, and Natural History. With Illustrations. 3 vols. Medium 8vo. 5*l.* 5*s.*

CONCISE BIBLE DICTIONARY. Condensed from the above. With Maps and 300 Illustrations. (1030 pp.) Medium 8vo. 21*s.*

SMALLER BIBLE DICTIONARY. Abridged from the above. With Maps and 40 Illustrations. (620 pp.) Crown 8vo. 7*s.* 6*d.*

DICTIONARY OF CHRISTIAN ANTIQUITIES. The History, Institutions, and Antiquities, from the Time of the Apostles to the Age of Charlemagne. With Illustrations. Vol. 1. (910 pp.) Medium 8vo. 31*s.* 6*d.*

DICTIONARY OF CHRISTIAN BIOGRAPHY, Literature, Sects, and Doctrines. From the Time of the Apostles to the Age of Charlemagne. Vol. I. (930 pp.) Medium 8vo. 31*s.* 6*d.*

DICTIONARY OF GREEK AND ROMAN ANTIQUITIES. Including the Laws, Institutions, Domestic Usages, Painting, Sculpture, Music, the Drama, &c. With 500 Illustrations. (1300 pp.) Medium 8vo. 28*s.*

DICTIONARY OF GREEK AND ROMAN BIOGRAPHY AND MYTHOLOGY. Containing a History of the Ancient World, civil, literary, and ecclesiastical. With 564 Illustrations. (3720 pp.) 3 Vols. Medium 8vo. 84*s.*

DICTIONARY OF GREEK AND ROMAN GEOGRAPHY. Including the political history of both countries and cities. With 530 Illustrations. (2512 pp.) 2 Vols. Medium 8vo. 56*s.*

CLASSICAL DICTIONARY OF MYTHOLOGY, BIOGRAPHY, AND GEOGRAPHY. With 750 Woodcuts. (840 pp.) 8vo. 18*s.*

SMALLER CLASSICAL DICTIONARY. With 200 Woodcuts. (472 pp.) Crown 8vo. 7*s.* 6*d.*

SMALLER DICTIONARY OF GREEK AND ROMAN ANTIQUITIES. With 200 Woodcuts. (474 pp.) Crown 8vo. 7*s.* 6*d.*

COMPLETE LATIN-ENGLISH DICTIONARY. With Tables of the Roman Calendar, Measures, Weights, and Moneys. (1220 pp.) Medium 8vo. 21*s.*

SMALLER LATIN-ENGLISH DICTIONARY: with Dictionary of Proper Names and Tables of Roman Calendar, etc. (672 pp.) Square 12mo. 7*s.* 6*d.*

COPIOUS & CRITICAL ENGLISH-LATIN DICTIONARY. (976 pp.) Medium 8vo. 21*s.*

SMALLER ENGLISH-LATIN DICTIONARY. (720 pp.) Square 12mo. 7*s.* 6*d.*

DR. WM. SMITH'S EDUCATIONAL COURSE.

"The general excellence of the books included in Mr. Murray's educational series, is so universally acknowledged as to give in a great degree the stamp of merit to the works of which it consists.—*Schoolmaster*."

LATIN COURSE.

PRINCIPIA LATINA, PART I. FIRST LATIN COURSE. A Grammar, Delectus, and Exercise Book with Vocabularies. (200 pp.) 12mo. 3s. 6d.

*** This work contains the Accidence arranged as in the "ORDINARY GRAMMARS" as well as in the "PUBLIC SCHOOLS LATIN PRIMER."

APPENDIX TO PRINCIPIA LATINA. PART I.; being Additional Exercises, with Examination Papers. 12mo. 2s. 6d.

PRINCIPIA LATINA, PART II. READING BOOK. An Introduction to Ancient Mythology, Geography, Roman Antiquities, and History. With Notes and a Dictionary. (268 pp.) 12mo. 3s. 6d.

PRINCIPIA LATINA, PART III. POETRY. 1. Easy Hexameters and Pentameters. 2. Eclogæ Ovidianæ. 3. Prosody and Metre. 4. First Latin Verse Book. (160 pp.) 12mo. 3s. 6d.

PRINCIPIA LATINA, PART IV. PROSE COMPOSITION. Rules of Syntax, with Examples, Explanations of Synonyms, and Exercises on the Syntax. (194 pp.) 12mo. 3s. 6d.

PRINCIPIA LATINA, PART V. SHORT TALES AND ANECDOTES FROM ANCIENT HISTORY, FOR TRANSLATION INTO LATIN PROSE. (140 pp.) 12mo. 3s.

LATIN-ENGLISH VOCABULARY, arranged according to Subjects and Etymology; with a Latin-English Dictionary to Phædrus, Cornelius Nepos, and Cæsar's "Gallic War." (190 pp.) 12mo. 3s. 6d.

THE STUDENT'S LATIN GRAMMAR. FOR THE HIGHER FORMS. (406 pp.) Post 8vo. 6s.

SMALLER LATIN GRAMMAR. Abridged from the above. (220 pp.) 12mo. 3s. 6d.

TACITUS. GERMANIA, AGRICOLA, AND FIRST BOOK OF THE ANNALS. With English Notes. (378 pp.) 12mo. 3s. 6d.

A CHILD'S FIRST LATIN BOOK, Including a Systematic Treatment of the NEW PRONUNCIATION; and PRAXIS OF NOUNS, ADJECTIVES, and PRONOUNS. By T. D. HALL, M.A. (68 pp.) 16mo.

GERMAN COURSE.

GERMAN PRINCIPIA, PART I. FIRST GERMAN COURSE. Containing Grammar, Delectus, Exercises, and Vocabulary. (164 pp.) 12mo. 3s. 6d.

GERMAN PRINCIPIA, PART II. A READING BOOK. Containing Fables, Stories, and Anecdotes, Natural History, and Scenes from the History of Germany. With Grammatical Questions, Notes, and Dictionary. (272 pp.) 12mo. 3s. 6d.

PRACTICAL GERMAN GRAMMAR. With a Sketch of the Historical Development of the Language and its Principal Dialects. (240 pp.) Post 8vo. 3s. 6d.

DR. WM. SMITH'S EDUCATIONAL COURSE.

GREEK COURSE.

INITIA GRÆCA, Part I. First Greek Course, containing Grammar, Delectus, Exercise Book, and Vocabularies. (104 pp.) 12mo. 3s. 6d.

INITIA GRÆCA, Part II. Reading Book; containing short Tales, Anecdotes, Fables, Mythology, and Grecian History. With a Lexicon. (220 pp.) 12mo. 3s. 6d.

INITIA GRÆCA, Part III. Prose Composition; containing the Rules of Syntax, with copious Examples and Exercises. (210 pp.) 12mo. 3s. 6d.

STUDENT'S GREEK GRAMMAR FOR THE Higher Forms. By Professor Curtius. (386 pp.) Post 8vo. 6s.

SMALLER GREEK GRAMMAR. Abridged from the above work. (220 pp.) 12mo. 3s. 6d.

GREEK ACCIDENCE. Extracted from the above work. (125 pp.) 12mo. 2s. 6d.

ELUCIDATIONS OF CURTIUS' GREEK GRAMMAR. Translated by Evelyn Abbott, M.A. Post 8vo. 7s. 6d.

PLATO. The Apology of Socrates, the Crito, and Part of the Phædo; with Notes in English from Stallbaum and Schleiermacher's Introductions. (242 pp.) 12mo. 3s. 6d.

FRENCH COURSE.

FRENCH PRINCIPIA, Part I. First French Course, containing Grammar, Delectus, Exercise Book, and Vocabularies. (180 pp.) 12mo. 3s. 6d.

FRENCH PRINCIPIA, Part II. Reading-Book, containing Fables, Stories, and Anecdotes, Natural History, and Scenes from the History of France. With Grammatical Questions, Notes, and a copious Etymological Dictionary. (364 pp.) 12mo. 4s. 6d.

FRENCH PRINCIPIA, Part III. Prose Composition, containing a systematic Course of Exercises on the Syntax with the Principal Rules of Syntax. 12mo. [*In the press.*

THE STUDENT'S FRENCH GRAMMAR: a Practical and Historical Grammar of the French Language. By C. Heron-Wall. With an Introduction by M. Littré. (490 pp.) Post 8vo. 7s. 6d.

A SMALLER GRAMMAR OF THE FRENCH LANGUAGE. For the Middle and Lower Forms. Abridged from the above. (230 pp.) 12mo. 3s. 6d.

ITALIAN COURSE.

ITALIAN PRINCIPIA. Part I. A First Italian Course, containing a Grammar, Delectus, Exercise Book, with Vocabularies, and Materials for Italian Conversation. By Signor Ricci. 12mo.

DR. WM. SMITH'S EDUCATIONAL COURSE.

ENGLISH COURSE.

PRIMARY HISTORY OF BRITAIN. FOR ELEMENTARY SCHOOLS. (368 pp.) 12mo. 2s. 6d.

"An admirable work, one of the best short school histories of England we have seen."—*Educational Times.*

SCHOOL MANUAL OF ENGLISH GRAMMAR; with Copious Exercises. By WM. SMITH, D.C.L., and T. D. HALL, M.A. (256 pp.) Post 8vo. 3s. 6d.

"The use of this book will render unnecessary that of many others. It is really a serviceable school-book."—*Nonconformist.*

PRIMARY ENGLISH GRAMMAR FOR ELEMENTARY SCHOOLS. With Exercises and Questions. Based upon the above work. By T. D. HALL, M.A. (76 pp.) 16mo. 1s.

"We doubt whether any grammar could be more clear, concise, and full than this."—*Watchman.*

A SCHOOL MANUAL OF ENGLISH COMPOSITION. With Copious Illustrations and Practical Exercises. By T. D. HALL. 12mo. [*In the Press.*

SCHOOL MANUAL OF MODERN GEOGRAPHY, PHYSICAL AND POLITICAL. By JOHN RICHARDSON, M.A. (400 pp.) Post 8vo. 5s.

"The most comprehensive, accurate, and methodical geography with which we are familiar."—*School Guardian.*

STANDARD SCHOOL BOOKS.

KING EDWARD VI.'s LATIN GRAMMAR; or, An Introduction to the Latin Tongue. (324 pp.) 12mo. 3s. 6d.

KING EDWARD VI.'s FIRST LATIN BOOK. THE LATIN ACCIDENCE. Syntax and Prosody, with an ENGLISH TRANSLATION. (220 pp.) 12mo. 2s. 6d.

OXENHAM'S ENGLISH NOTES FOR LATIN ELEGIACS, designed for early proficients in the art of Latin Versification. (156 pp.) 12mo. 3s. 6d.

HUTTON'S PRINCIPIA GRÆCA. AN INTRODUCTION TO THE STUDY OF GREEK. A Grammar, Delectus, and Exercise Book, with Vocabularies. (154 pp.) 12mo. 3s. 6d.

MATTHIÆ'S GREEK GRAMMAR. Abridged by BLOMFIELD. Revised by E. S. CROOKE, B.A. (412 pp.) Post 8vo. 4s.

LEATHES' HEBREW GRAMMAR. With the Hebrew text of Genesis i.—vi., and Psalms i.—vi. Grammatical Analysis and Vocabulary. (252 pp.) Post 8vo. 7s. 6d.

MRS. MARKHAM'S HISTORIES.

"Mrs. Markham's Histories are constructed on a plan which is novel and we think well chosen, and we are glad to find that they are deservedly popular, for they cannot be too strongly recommended."—*Journal of Education.*

A HISTORY OF ENGLAND, FROM THE FIRST INVASION BY THE ROMANS. By MRS. MARKHAM. Continued down to 1867. With Conversations at the end of each Chapter. With 100 Woodcuts. (528 pp.) 12mo. 3s. 6d.

A HISTORY OF FRANCE, FROM THE CONQUEST BY THE GAULS. By MRS. MARKHAM. Continued down to 1861. With Conversations at the end of each Chapter. With 70 Woodcuts. (550 pp.) 12mo. 3s. 6d.

A HISTORY OF GERMANY, FROM THE INVASION OF THE KINGDOM BY THE ROMANS UNDER MARIUS. On the plan of MRS. MARKHAM. Continued down to 1867. With 50 Woodcuts. (460 pp.) 12mo. 3s. 6d.

LITTLE ARTHUR'S HISTORY OF ENGLAND. By LADY CALLCOTT. Continued down to the year 1872. With 36 Woodcuts. (286 pp.) 16mo. 1s. 6d.

"I never met with a history so well adapted to the capacities of children or their entertainment, so philosophical, and written with such simplicity."—*Mrs. Marcett.*

ÆSOP'S FABLES. A New Version. By THOS. JAMES, M.A. With 100 Woodcuts. (168 pp.) Post 8vo. 2s. 6d.

"Of ÆSOP'S FABLES there ought to be in every school many copies, full of pictures."—*Fraser's Magazine.*

THE BIBLE IN THE HOLY LAND: BEING EXTRACTS FROM DEAN STANLEY'S SINAI AND PALESTINE. With Woodcuts. (210 pp.) 16mo. 2s. 6d.

NATURAL PHILOSOPHY & SCIENCE.

NEWTH'S FIRST BOOK OF NATURAL PHILOSOPHY; an Introduction to the Study of Statics, Dynamics, Hydrostatics, Light, Heat, and Sound, with numerous Examples. *New and enlarged edition.* Small 8vo. 3s. 6d.

NEWTH'S ELEMENTS OF MECHANICS, including Hydrostatics, with numerous Examples. (374 pp.) Small 8vo. 8s. 6d.

NEWTH'S MATHEMATICAL EXAMPLES. A Graduated Series of Elementary Examples in Arithmetic, Algebra, Logarithms, Trigonometry, and Mechanics. (378 pp.) Small 8vo. 8s. 6d.

JOHN MURRAY, ALBEMARLE STREET.

Bradbury, Agnew, & Co., Printers, Whitefriars.

CPSIA information can be obtained
at www.ICGtesting.com
Printed in the USA
LVHW081024180722
723704LV00024B/407